PSYCHOANALYSIS PHILOSOPHIES AND PRACTICES

DR. JIPSON LAWRANCE J

ISBN 979-888530974-5

I dedicate this book to my beloved parents and brother, those who made me become an educationalist and a writer.

Contents

FOREWORD

Professional counselors use a variety of therapies in their work, and there are hundreds of clinical counseling options available to you. The most recent SAGE Encyclopedia of Theory in Counseling and Psychotherapy lists over 300 different ways to make counseling. So how do counselors know which method is best for them? To answer that question, we first need to understand that there is no better way to counsel. That is because counseling methods are based on theories about human performance and change as opposed to strong evidence.

Determining whether one form of counseling works better than another is difficult, since there are many variables that must be considered in the counseling process. For example, if we try to compare the effectiveness of two counselors using the same theoretical model, there may be significant differences in counseling outcomes due to differences in client histories and circumstances, differences in counselor communication methods, and even differences. in the case of a client and a consultant on the date of the comparison.

Such a difference is difficult to control by testing, thus it is almost impossible to prove that one method of counseling is the best option. Without such evidence, it is the responsibility of counselors to do everything possible to ensure that the treatment model (s) they use are best suited to address the needs of each client. That responsibility begins with getting acquainted with models that have proved to be very useful in real life.

PREFACE

Psychoanalysis Philosophies and Practices is a guide to effective work in the psychologist, either as a student, teacher, or researcher. It aims to accompany you throughout the process in developing, conducting, and reporting psychological research.

As the book deals mainly with psychology students and researchers, many sections are written as a step-by-step manual to guide the student through the various activities that take place during the test. Due to the structure of the general sequence of events that took place during the study (designing informed consent forms and discussion papers, obtaining approval from the institutional review board, or the like), they can be easily used as additional learning materials in practical psychological assessment studies. .

ACKNOWLEDGEMENTS

Writing a book is harder than I thought and more rewarding than I could have ever imagined. None of this would have been possible without my dearest parents and brother. My brother Lickson Lawrence was the first friend I made when I stepped in to this world. He stood by me during every struggle and all my successes.

I'm eternally grateful to my father, Dr.D.E.Lawrance, who took in an extra mouth to feed when he didn't have to. He taught me discipline, tough love, manners, respect, and so much more that has helped me succeed in life. I truly have no idea where I'd be if he hadn't given me a roof over my head or become the father whom I desperately needed at that age.

To my mother Mrs.Jaya Lawrence, who took a chance on a kid and let him chase his dreams. She never saw my age, my fight, or my lack of formal lifestyle. She just saw a kid hungry to learn, hungry to grow, and hungry to succeed in life. She never stopped me; she only encouraged me.

Although this period of my life was filled with many ups and downs. My time in the world wouldn't have been made possible without my parents who taught me the honest life's game.

A very special thanks to Dr.Stalin K Thomas Internatonal Director of IATA. Thank you for always encouraging me to stick to academic writings.

Writing a book about the human mind is a surreal process. I'm forever indebted to all for their help, keen insight, and ongoing support in bringing my writings.

To everyone at the Notion press who enables me to be the writer of a book. I'm honored to be a part of Notion Press Publishing Company, thank you for letting me in, for being a part of amazing world of writers.

Finally, to all those who have been a part of my life's journey

Thank You

PROLOGUE

Psychoanalysis Philosophies and Practices provide a framework for therapists and counselors to interpret client behavior, thoughts, and feelings and help them navigate the client's journey from diagnosis to treatment or well-being. Theoretical methods are an integral part of the healing process. But with so many different options out there, how do you know which method of counseling works best for you? Whether you are a student of counseling or a client looking for a qualified therapist, the following detailed explanations will give you a deeper understanding of each counseling theory and procedure. These ideas are incorporated into all reading

I

SLAB- I : (COUNSELLING – HOLISTIC PERSPECTIVE) Introduction

Counseling is a one-on-one relationship that involves a qualified counselor and focuses on other aspects of client adjustment, development needs, or decision-making. This process provides the basis for relationships and communication in which the client can develop understanding, explore potential and initiate change.

In this case, the power of the counselors makes the best results. The skills and knowledge of counselors provide the right framework and guidance that enhances the client's capacity for effective outcomes.

COUNSELLING IS A PROCESS

Start of counseling session (Introduction): As the client enters the room, greet the person, call the person by name, welcome the client, and make him or her feel comfortable. Let yourself know when you meet for the first time and tell the person the purpose of the meeting (understanding the health problem and its best management). Encourage the counselor to talk about them.

Attendance and Active Listening: It is a very important step of counseling because the information provided to the client is based on it. Active listening means paying close attention and paying attention to oral and non-verbal signals. Provide in-depth information to relieve client fears and anxieties. Similarly, the words, speeches, and posture of the counselor (verbal/non-verbal communication) show attention to what is being said. By demonstrating the behavior of visiting the client self-esteem is enhanced, and it creates a safe environment and helps to express the idea freely by the counselor. Active listening involves expressing emotions, asking questions, summarizing words, and expressing oneself. Similarly, the actions of a mentor convey many emotions that are not expressed. Some of these trivial tasks are room-assisted counseling, Voice Quality, Breathing, Eyes, Face Condition, Leg Movement & Bodybuilding.

Content Display and Emotions: People react differently to their situations. They may express their feelings such as fear, anger, anxiety, or sadness about the disease. Eg. Depression can be manifested as short-term irritability, irritable behavior, little interest in the daily routine, inability to sleep, weight loss, and feelings of worthlessness and anxiety. Do not try to stop, let the person express his or her feelings, do not prevent the patient/ family members from crying. Do not hold a grudge and try to stay calm.

The counselor must be sensitive to such feelings in a positive, emotional way. Focus is maintained on the client's emotions and his or her coping experience. The counselor reflects the content and feelings of other people by responding to the client and conveying a message with empathy, asking questions, or summarizing that the counselor is listening and trying to understand the counselor's circumstances.

Asking: Always try to use questions and establish connections so that both problem and solutions are clear. Ask questions to clarify the situation

and make the client aware of all aspects of the problem and help the client understand the context that is causing his or her fears or concerns. Do not ask too many closed questions (closed questions are questions that can be answered in one word such as yes / no). Ask open-ended questions to make communication easier, encourage continuous communication, and encourage building trust and warmth in relationships.

Use questions that contain why with caution as it may sound like judgment. If you need to use the word —why‖, use it during the sentence and not at the beginning of the sentence.

Briefness and clarity: A humorous repetition of a customer's feelings made by the counselor in his own words. For example, —It looks like you are afraid your family will not take care of you‖. Customers may agree with the description. If not, the counselor may need clarification on —would you like to explain more? Sebenzisa Using this method, the counselor tries to provide feedback to the client; the context or content of what the client has just said and clarifies understanding the client's world. Clarification helps the client to understand themselves better. If you ask a client to explain something in detail or in a different way; in this way, clients not only assess their feelings continuously but will also feel that you are trying hard to understand their situation. In this program, counselors also tell the client about scientific facts they do not know.

Definition: People usually avoid focusing on the real problem and talking about the matter. Interpretation goes beyond what is clearly stated by the feelings and meanings expressed by client statements. Even the client does not know this. The Counselor redefines the problem with a different perspective to bring more clarity to the problem and make the client aware of the underlying problem. The counselor also helps the client find out what is appropriate, emphasizing key points - for example, — Of all the things you talked about today, it seems to me that you are very worried .... ‖

Recurrence: In times of stress and stress, clients are in a state of denial or feel frustrated. They may not always understand everything they are told. As a counselor, do not hesitate to repeat important points of discussion, supporting statements, or facts needed. It ensures that clients clearly understand the problem and the necessary action. The client will usually show that they understand and accept the information.

Summary: Many people who are surprised by the news of the disease may respond by speaking quickly and trying to provide more details or ask more questions; instead the counselor may suck or understand you. Then it helps the counselor to interrupt from time to time and summarize what has been said. This is similar to summarizing and helps to ensure that each understands the other correctly. Summary at the end of the counseling provides guidance and direction for both the counselor and the counselor; to address the actual issues of the problem and determine the application. A summary is like a combination of emotional expressions and long phrases.

At the end of each session, the facilitator should summarize the main points of the discussion, highlighting the decisions made and the need for action.

Conflict: Often clients who are too busy with their fears may not be able to see the connection between their behavior and the responses of others. Conflict involves a direct assessment of the conflict of interest in the thoughts, feelings, and/or behavior of the client. The counselor tells the client how his or her thoughts affect his or her action and behavior, which in turn affects the behavior of others in it. Eg. Because of fear of stigma, people withdraw from contact with friends and relatives. Friends and relatives too react in unfavorable circumstances. Establishing strong relationships and understanding is important before commenting on such issues. It is a very limited skill which is why time is so important and advice to deal with it should be given in a warm, caring, and caring environment.

Respect: As a counselor, try to acknowledge that people perceive their problems in different ways that are determined by culture, social class, and personality. Respect clients' ideas and beliefs and build on them. Show respect, for example, by asking the client to explain various aspects of your culture or beliefs that are unfamiliar to you; for example, —you feel powerful about this. I don't know about it. Tell me more about it ‖.

Planning or prioritization: Planning means helping the client see the relationship between facts and feelings. Helps clients identify important aspects of their concerns that need immediate attention and other less important issues that can be postponed until later. It is an important part of planning and probably one of the most important skills in counseling.

Application Determination: Based on the scientific knowledge, cultural and socio-economic aspects of the client, help the client explore all possible solutions for the priority factor and choose the most appropriate option. Encourage clients to make their own decisions and act accordingly.

Concluding counseling session: At the end of the session summarize the key points and decisions taken, congratulate the clients on their efforts, wish them luck and arrange a follow-up visit.

PURPOSE AND GOALS OF COUNSELLING

The goal of counseling is to help people overcome their problems quickly and to equip them to deal with future problems. Counseling, for purpose, should be clear to each client as it involves their unique problems and expectations. Counseling policies can be defined as immediate, long-term, and procedural principles. A goal statement is not only important but also necessary because it gives a sense of direction and purpose. Additionally, it is necessary for a rational evaluation of its use.

The counselor aims to understand the behavior, motives, and feelings of the counselor/client. The mentor's goals are not limited to understanding his clients. You have different goals at different levels of performance. The immediate goal is to get the client help and the long-term goal is to make him a 'fully functional person. Both immediate and long-term goals are protected by what is known as mediation or procedural principles.

Specific counseling policies are different for each client and include consideration of client expectations and environmental factors. Apart from certain terms, there are two main categories of policies in most counseling cases. These are identified as long-distance policies and procedures. The latter is of great importance. They build relationships and behaviors of counselors and mentors. The principles of the procedure include helpful procedures to improve the effectiveness of counseling.

Long-term goals are those that reflect the philosophy of life counselor and can be said to be -

i. Helping the mentor do what he or she wants

ii. Helping the mentor gain self-awareness

iii. Helping the mentor become a fully functional person.

Immediate counseling guidelines refer to problems the client seeks solutions to here and now. A mentor can be helped to gain a full understanding by examining himself and appreciating his strengths and weaknesses. A counselor can provide the necessary information but no matter how complete, it may not be helpful to the client unless they have a comprehensive understanding of themselves, their own resources, and environmental issues and resources.

There is a connection between long-term and immediate goals as both depend on the objectives of the process to achieve them. The principles of the process are basic counseling standards which are essential conditions for counseling to take place. They incorporate a sympathetic, warm, and friendly understanding that provides a personal evaluation that also assists the client in self-evaluation and self-understanding and ultimately leads to long-term goals namely self-efficacy, self-efficacy, and self-improvement.

Discussing the objectives of counseling, Parloff (1961) distinguishes between immediate and final principles according to which the first refers to the steps and stages of the counseling process that lead to the attainment of final goals. Patterson (1970) proposes a third level of goals i.e. middle goals in addition to mediation and end goals. The latter goals refer to the broad and general long-term outcomes such as well mental health. The intermediate goals are defined by the reasons for seeking counseling and immediate goals such as those that refer to the current counselor's intentions. The biggest criticism expressed is that goals such as self-realization, realism, etc., are very common and have not changed so they do not apply to real practice. Krumboltz (1966) argues that the working definition of terms can be a very useful method. He suggests that common sense can be reduced to a specific purpose and measurable variables. Mediation objectives (Parloff, 1967) can be considered as specific steps that contribute to the achievement of common goals. Behavioralists place great emphasis on mediation goals such as reducing anxiety, finding behavioral patterns, etc. The immediate goal of counseling is to encourage the potential counselor to make time for the counselor and to undertake the counseling process until the mediation objectives are met. It is through the achievement of mediation goals that the ultimate goals of self-realization, self-realization - self-realization, and self-realization can be achieved. The self-assessment process is probably the kind of immediate goal that sets the process for counseling to continue. Areas where change is considered desirable relationships with other people, academic success, job satisfaction, etc. Some of the main principles of counseling commonly accepted by counselors are given below: -

1. The success of good mental health

It is considered an important goal of counseling by some people who say that when a person achieves good mental health he learns to adapt and respond well to people and situations. Kell and Mueller (1962) state that —The promotion and development of feelings of love, sharing and receiving and providing communication rewards from other people is a legitimate purpose for counseling‖.

2. Problem Solving

Another purpose of counseling is to resolve the issue raised by the counselor. This, in fact, is the result of an earlier purpose and means better mental health. Behaviorally can be seen three stages of ethical goals, namely, reversing bad behavior, learning the decision-making process, and preventing problems (Krumboltz, 1966).

3. Improving Personal Performance

However, another goal of counseling is to improve personal efficiency. This is closely related to maintaining good mental health and achieving desirable behavioral changes.

4. Change Assistance Advice

Blocher (1966) added two more goals. First, he said, counseling should increase individual freedom of choice and act in accordance with environmental requirements. Another goal is that counseling should increase the effectiveness of individual responses from the environment. Tiedeman, (1964) argues that the purpose of counseling is to focus on the path of change and that the counselor should be assisted in the process of becoming a full-fledged change during adolescence in which the person is assisted. to fulfill his potential. Shoben (1965) also views the purpose of counseling as personal development.

5. Decision-Making - Acting as a Counseling Goal

Some counselors feel that counseling should help the counselor to make decisions. Terms of Advice. The goal of counseling is to help people overcome their problems quickly and to equip them to deal with future problems. Counseling, for purpose, should be clear to each client as it involves their unique problems and expectations. Counseling policies can be defined as immediate, long-term, and procedural principles. A goal statement is not only important but also necessary because it gives a sense of direction and purpose.

Additionally, it is necessary for a rational evaluation of its use.

The counselor has the goal of understanding the behavior, motives, and feelings of the counselor. A consultant has goals that are not limited to understanding his or her clients. You have different goals at different levels of performance. The immediate goal is to get client help and the long-term goal is to make him or her a full-time employee. Both immediate and long-term goals are protected by what is known as mediation or procedural principles.

Specific counseling policies are different for each client and include consideration of client expectations and environmental factors. Apart from certain terms, there are two main categories of policies in most counseling cases. These are identified as long-distance policies and procedures. The latter is of great importance. They build relationships and behaviors of counselors and mentors. The principles of the procedure include helpful procedures to improve the effectiveness of counseling. Long-term goals are those that reflect the philosophy of life counselor and can be said to be

1. Help the mentor to do what he or she wants.
2. Helping the counselor gain self-awareness.
3. Helping the mentor become a fully functional person.

Immediate counseling guidelines refer to problems the client seeks solutions to here and now. A mentor can be helped to gain a full understanding by examining himself and appreciating his strengths and weaknesses. A counselor can provide the necessary information but no matter how complete, it may not be helpful to the client unless they have a comprehensive understanding of themselves, their own resources, and environmental issues and resources.

There is a connection between long-term and immediate goals as both depend on the objectives of the process to achieve them. The principles of the process are basic counseling standards which are essential conditions for counseling to take place. They incorporate a sympathetic, warm, and friendly understanding that provides a personal evaluation that also assists the client in self-evaluation and self-understanding and ultimately leads to long-term goals namely self-efficacy, self-efficacy, and self-improvement.

6. Behavioral Change As a Goal

Behavioral-focused counselors emphasize the need for behavioral change, for example, the removal of unwanted behavior or action or the reduction of an annoying sign in order to achieve satisfaction and effectiveness. Growth-focused mentors emphasize the development of strength within the person. Existing counselors emphasize self-improvement and self-fulfillment. Clearly, the latter will not be possible without first acquisition, that is, the removal of symptoms or a reduction as a prerequisite for personal success.

The general public tends to view counseling as a corrective action and emphasizes immediate goals, such as problem-solving, conflict resolution, and the like. A counselor may refer to a solution to a dispute or to a situation.

However, the purpose of counseling is appropriately related to basic and fundamental factors such as self-awareness and self-realization. This service provides the mentor with guidance and encouragement. Emotional and psychological counseling are fruitful. It aims to help a person develop in such a way that they can grow mentally and be able to fully realize their potential.

Counseling has no magical solution. The only logical, sensible and realistic view of counseling is that it is not and cannot be everything to everyone. It is about helping individuals find practical and practical solutions to their problems by helping them to see for themselves so that they can use their skills and opportunities and thus become independent, self-reliant, and self-reliant. It is a process of critical decisions in which human growth is encouraged. Reaves and Reaves (1965) state that the main purpose of counseling is to encourage people to evaluate, act, accept and act on their own initiative.

Sometimes counselors have vague intentions and their effects are not fully appreciated. Perhaps one of the main functions of a counselor is to help determine the purpose of the counselor.

OVERVIEW STAGES OF COUNSELLING

Hackney and Cormier, (1996) have presented the following categories of counseling as follows:

2. Establishment of relationships
3. Problem identification and evaluation
4. Planning to solve problems
5. Solution, application, and termination

1. Establishment of relationships

Counseling is a supportive relationship. The counselor must take the initiative in initiating a dialogue to establish a climate that allows for mutual respect, trust, open and free communication, and a broad understanding of what the consultation process involves.

Although the obligation will eventually grow to the client, at this stage the responsibility for the counseling process lies with the counselor. Among the methods a counselor may use are those designed to relieve tension and communicate openly. Both the mentor's attitude and verbal communication are essential to the development of a satisfying relationship. In the latter case, all of the counselor's communication skills such as careful listening, understanding, and feeling with the client are used.

Conditions such as good manners and courtesy, accurate empathy, and sincerity mean the ease of counseling, the ability to understand and understand the client, and to value the client. The counselor's relationship with the client not only increases the chances of the clients achieving their goals but also is a possible model of positive interpersonal relationships, which clients can use to improve the quality of their relationships without medical treatment.

The counseling process within these relationships seeks to assist the client in taking responsibility for their problem and its solution. This will be facilitated by the counselor's communication skills, the ability to see and express the client's feelings, and the ability to identify and gain an understanding of the client's concerns and needs. Suggested terms for initial counseling discussions may include:

Terms of advisor

- Build positive and comfortable relationships
- Explain the counseling process and the obligations of both clients
- Facilitate communication
- Identify and confirm the client's concerns that led him or her to seek counseling
- Plan, with the client, to get the test data needed to proceed with the counseling process

Client Terms

- Understand the mentoring process and its responsibilities in the program
- Share and expand on reasons for seeking advice
- Collaborate on exploring both the problem and you

2. Problem Detection and Assessment

Once a sufficient relationship has been established, clients will be more receptive to in-depth discussion and concerns that concern them. At this stage, clients take on more responsibility because it is their problem and it is their willingness to discuss as much of the problem with the counselor as possible that will determine to the maximum extent the assistance the counselor can provide.

During this phase, the counselor continues to demonstrate the behavior of the visitor and can specifically emphasize communication skills such as summarizing, clarifying, evaluating an idea or response. The counselor may ask the client, but the questions are explained in such a way as to facilitate the further assessment of the client's concerns. Questions that may embarrass, challenge or threaten the client are avoided. Throughout this phase, the facilitator will be able to identify cultural differences and their implications for how strategies should be changed to be culturally appropriate.

Now the consultant wants to distinguish between what might be called external problems and the most complex ones. The counselor also tries to determine if the problem is, in fact, a concern that has brought the client to the counselor. This can be a time for information collection. The most useful information a counselor has will be more likely to accurately assess client needs. It is therefore helpful for advisers to identify the various areas of information that need to be activated.

Information may be collected under the following three headings:

1. The amount of time covers a client's experience, especially what he or she might consider being an influential experience. The current size will include how well the person is doing right now, especially those current events that may be causing the client to seek counseling. Future plans will include future prospects, plans, and goals, as well as how the client plans to achieve this.

2. The magnitude of the emotion encompasses the client's feelings and feelings towards him or her and others who are important. Included are feelings about groups, attitudes, values, and personal opinions. They are all part of the greatness of the feeling.

3. The greatness of the concept includes how the client solves problems, the coping styles he or she uses, the rationality in daily decision-making, and the strength and readiness to learn.

At this point, some counselors may use diagnostic techniques as a standard diagnostic test. Minor problematic issues can also be identified.

During this phase, the client not only assesses the experience and behavior but can also express feelings and relationships of concern in the way he or she lives in general. The consultant wants to protect as much relevant data as possible and associate it with a complete picture of the client and her concerns. The counselor also shares these ideas with the client. The goal of this section is for the counselor and client to see the problem and its consequences in the same way. One of the counselors' goals in this phase is to help the client understand that he or she sees the need to deal with anxiety - the need for change and action.

The steps or stages of problem identification and testing are:

1. Explain the problem - The counselor, in collaboration with the client, wants to explain or point out the problem as directly and indirectly as possible. It is important that the counselor and the client have the same understanding of the problem. In addition to the desired accuracy in describing the problem, it is important for the client to identify the components or features that contribute and the magnitude of the problem in terms of its occurrence and longevity.

2. Assess the problem - The types of information needed to fully understand the problem and its background are collected at this point, Once the required types of information have been identified, the consultant and client must decide how this information can be obtained, who is responsible for collecting it, and what will be the data collection times. Within this context, decisions can be made about the management, for example, of common psychological measures. Whether or not to test is a decision where the client should have a loud voice. No matter how desirable it is to obtain data through common psychological measures, the outcome for the client and his or her willingness to participate fully in the counseling process may be threatened by this data collection process. In some cases, a counselor may wish to complete a detailed case study. This is a decision that will depend on the complexity of the situation, the amount of data required, and the time available to both counselor and client for this purpose. In this program, it is clear that it is important for the counselor to continue to use the intervention method.

3. Gather information - At this point all the information collected is systematically organized and integrated with a reasonable client profile and client problem. At this point, it may be appropriate to begin examining the

changes that may be needed and the potential barriers to these changes.

3. Planning to solve problems

Once the consultant has determined that all the important information about a client's concerns is available and understandable and once the client has accepted the need to do something about a particular problem, it is time to devise a strategy to resolve or resolve the client's concerns. client.

At this point, setting the outcome of the outcome becomes the essence of the counseling task. Errors in setting policies can lead to unproductive practices and the client loses confidence in the counseling process.

1. Explain the problem - It is important that the counselor and client look at the problem from the same perspective and have the same understanding of its consequences.

2. Find and write down all possible solutions - At this point, it is advisable to consult by all means. Both the client and the consultant share, but the client should be given the opportunity to write down as many things as may come to mind. If there are obvious solutions that are ignored, the counselor may suggest to the client,

‖Have you ever thought of __? ‖ When writing solutions, nothing should be removed simply because at first glance it seems impossible.

3. Evaluate the results of the proposed solutions - Here the client with the occasional encouragement and suggestions of the consultant will identify the processes needed to implement each of the proposed solutions. As he does so, some processes will seem more complicated or for other reasons impossible. Some solutions may produce more problems or worse effects than the problem focused on this series of counseling. In any case, the proposed results of each solution should be carefully considered.

4. Prioritize Solutions - After the testing phase, the client, with the advice of a consultant, will prioritize solutions from the lowest possible down to the lowest chances of producing the desired results. Once the decision has been made and the best solution is selected, the client is now ready to proceed with the application and implementation.

In the ongoing development of this program, the counselor realizes that the client will often not come to the basic ideas, impacts, or possibilities as quickly as the counselor will approach. However, most counselors will agree that it is best to guide the client in achieving this understanding itself. To facilitate client understanding, the counselor may use repetition techniques, eye contact, translation, information, and motivation.

4 Solution, Application, and Termination

In this last step, the obligations are clear. The client is responsible for using the fixed solution, as well as the advisor, in deciding the termination point. In the first case, the counselor is responsible for promoting the client's action with a fixed problem solution. While the client is fully involved in applying the solution to the problem, the counselor will usually keep in touch as a source of follow-up, support, and encouragement. The client may also need the help of a counselor in case things go awry.

The obligation to terminate is primarily the advisor although the client had the right to terminate at any time. The counselor usually gives a signal that the next interview should be completed and may conclude by summarizing the main points of the counseling process. In most cases, the counselor will be open to possible client reinstatement if further assistance is required

The counselor hopes that the client has not only learned to deal with the specific problem but also learned problem-solving skills that will reduce the client's need for further counseling in the future.

It should be borne in mind that problems are not always based on what appears to be a defect or failure that requires repair and restorative treatment, clients may have equally stressful needs due to concerns about improving their human capacity - in order to use their potential. In these cases, emphasis is placed on development, growth, or development rather than remediation.

CHARACTERISTICS OF AN EFFECTIVE COUNSELLOR

The following are the personal qualities and characteristics that are essential for an effective counselor:

- *They have an identity.* They know who they are, what they are capable of becoming, what they want out of life, and what is essential.

- *Respect and appreciate themselves.* They can give andreceive help and love out of their own sense of self-worth and strength. They feel adequate with others and allow others to feel powerful with them

- *Are open to change.* They make decisions about how they would like to change, and they work toward becoming the person they want to become.
- *Make choices that are life-oriented.* They are aware of earlydecisions they made about themselves, others, and the world. They are not the victims of these early decisions, and they are willing to revise them if necessary.
- *Are authentic, sincere, and honest.* They don't hide behind masks,defenses. They are genuine
- *Have a sense of humor.* They have not forgotten how to laugh,especially at their own weaknesses and contradictions.
- *Make mistakes and are willing to admit them.* They don't dismiss their error slightly, yet they don't choose to worry about them forever.
- *Live in the present.* They are not fixed to thepast, no rare they fixated on the future. They are able to experience and be present with others in the—now.
- *Appreciate the influence of culture.* They are aware of theway in which their own culture affects them, and they respect the diversity of values of other cultures. They are also sensitive to the unique differences arising out of social class, race, sexual orientation, and gender
- *Have as in cere interest in the welfare of others.* This concern is based on respect, care, trust, and a real valuing of others.
- *Possess effective interpersonal skills.* They are capable of entering theworld of others without getting lost in this world, and they strive to create collaborative relationships with others.
- *Become deeply involved in their work and derive meaning from it.* They can accept the rewards flowing from their work, yet they are not slaves to their work.
- *Effective Counsellors are passionate.* They have the courage to pursue their passions, and they are passionate about life and their work(Skovholt& Jennings,2004).
- *Are able to maintain healthy boundaries.* Although theystrive to be fully present for their clients, they don't carry the problems of their clients around with them during leisure hours. They know how to say no, which enables them to maintain balance in their lives.

Combs (1989) reviewing 13 studies about effective and ineffective helping relationships, concluded that there are some shared beliefs among helpers in the major helping professions, such as:

1. Attitude toward other people: The effective helper views people as being able rather than unable, worthy rather than unworthy, dependable rather than undependable, helpful and friendly rather than hindering and alienating, optimistic about others rather than negative.
2. Self-concept: Effective helpers feel personally adequate rather than inadequate, identify with others rather than feel isolated, feel trustworthy rather than untrustworthy, feel wanted rather than unwanted, feel worthy rather than unworthy.
3. Approaches to helping: Effective helpers are more directed toward people than things and are more likely to approach clients subjectively or phenomenologically – that is, from the client's vantage point and perspective rather than from their own. The strategies that they use are implemented empathically and are congruent with their own values.

Rogers (1958) believes that counselors must be open and that the following conditions are necessary for client development in a helping relationship:

1. Unconditional Positive Regard: Counsellors should communicate acceptance of clients as worthwhile persons, regardless of who they are or what they say or do.
2. Genuineness and congruence: Counsellors should be real and sincere, honest and clear. They should speak and act congruently. They should practice what they preach.
3. Empathy: Counsellors should be able to communicate an empathic understanding of clients' frames of reference and should let them know they feel and understand clients' concerns from their point of view.

Carkhuff and Berenson (1967) identified four basic traits that facilitate effective helping relationships if communicated skillfully.

1. Empathy: Effective counselors are able to communicate to the client their own self-awareness and understanding, providing the client with an experiential base for change.
2. Respect and positive regard: Effective counselors can communicate warmth and care.
3. Genuineness: Effective counselors are honest with themselves and their clients.

4. Concreteness: Effective counselors respond accurately, clearly, specifically, and immediately to clients.

Corey (2001) implores counselors to learn about themselves as persons in the helping relationship. He stresses the following conditions:

1. Self-awareness: Counsellors should continuously develop their awareness of their own values and feelings in order to grow, be open to change, and model congruent behavior and high-risk activity. Self-awareness leads to greater authenticity.
2. Interest: Counsellors should show interest in and involvement with the welfare of others and the influence of culture on all people.
3. Knowledge and skills: In order to be professionally effective, practitioners need to be able to integrate psychological theory and practice into their personal meaning. They must integrate multicultural competencies into their knowledge and skills.

Sue and Sue (1999) summarized the following important characteristics of multiculturally competent counselors

1. Self-awareness: Counsellors should be aware of their own standards, values, and assumptions.

2. Knowledge: They need to be knowledgeable of the socio-political factors operating in their clients' worlds and know that they may inadvertently discriminate if they treat all clients alike.

3. Understanding: Counsellors need to be able to understand the worldview of each client.

Egan (1998) refines the concept of empathy by defining two types: primary empathy, in which counselors attend, listen and reflect to communicate an accurate perception of the client's message; and advanced accurate empathy, in which, in addition to communicating primary empathy, the counselor influences the client through self-disclosure, directives or interpretation.

Brammer believes that the following conditions are necessary to the effective helping relationship:

1. **Self-awareness:** Counsellors should be aware of their own values and feelings, of the use (and power) of their ability to function as models for the clients.

2. **Interest:** Counsellors should show interest in and involvement with people and social change

3. **Ethical behavior:** Counsellors should demonstrate commitment to behaviors that are reflections of their own moral standards, of society's codes, and of the norms of the helping profession.

Ivey, Ivey, and Simek-Downing (1997) and Ivey and Ivey (1999) have summarized the findings into what they consider to be the qualitative communication components necessary for effective helping.

1. Empathy (primary and advanced accurate)

2. Positive Regard – selectively attending to positive aspects of the client's verbalizations and behavior

3. Respect – stating positive opinions of the client and openly and honestly acknowledging, appreciating, and tolerating differences
4. Warmth – showing concern for the client through nonverbal expression

5. Concreteness – clarifying facts and feelings specifically
6. Immediacy – speaking in the present instead of the past or future tense

7. Confrontation – Discuss differences, mixed messages, incongruities, and discrepancies between verbal and nonverbal behaviors.

8. Genuineness – Being authentic, spontaneous, and sensitive to the needs of the client.

ETHICS IN COUNSELLING.

The Code of Conduct is intended to protect counselors in the community and vice versa and professional organizations such as the American Counseling Organization, the American Psychological Organization, and many other Indian professional organizations continue to update their code of conduct. Many codes of conduct are based on five fundamental principles: (1) respect independence (2) do not harm (3) benefit others (4) be impartial and (5) be honest (Kitchener, 1988).

Behavioral problems are becoming more complex and complex, and it is impossible for helpers to avoid them. Those whose behavior is consistent with their sense of helpfulness and who are not committed to questioning their own behavior and motives and seeking to consult with others are less likely to act improperly than those who are trapped in such thinking.

Moral issues that appear to be important in the present system are (1) specialized communication and the sharing of confidential information, especially in this age of supervision and high technology, (2) conflict of interest (3) record keeping (4) use of testing and computer programs (5) dual relationships and (6)) and distortion of facts.

Right Communication and Confidentiality

Some counselors are lucky enough to be in touch, which means they can be called to testify in a court of law about the nature of their conversation with clients and their records can be called. There are two types of confidentiality: legal and personal. The former depends on the laws of a particular country/country. The latter you made for yourself. In other words, if because of your condition (such as a school or correctional facility) you are unable to keep confidential information provided during a service, you should explain this to the client in advance about sharing it with you.

If you are able to promise a personal secret, you must keep it under any circumstances. Recent court cases show that professional assistants can be prosecuted if they do not warn potential victims of violence.

The best way for clients and clients to be protected is for clients to sign an informed consent form and for clients and clients to discuss openly what diagnostics will be used. Counselors are also responsible for ensuring that their employer's union policies comply with their employment and personal codes.

Conflicts of Interest

There are times when mentors may have a conflict of interest between their obligations to their organization and their obligations to their clients. There are no sleep solutions in such cases. Everyone has to find a way to live.

It is important for counselors to remember that their main function during the client-assisted process is, not for any other person or group, therefore, when a conflict of interest arises, counselors should ensure that they do not violate client law. confidentiality because of their ignorance, insecurity, or incompetence, or because of an organization or group. The only reason for the violation of privacy is that the welfare of the client or another person is in danger.

Record keeping

In the case of records, it may be a good idea to record the sole purpose, ethical information, and set aside personal property/explanations. When using audiocassettes, there should be complete customer information, a complete description of the purposes and objectives of the recording, and the advisor's assurance that the tapes will be destroyed after achieving their objectives. If third-party payments are involved, discuss what specific information is provided to that person. Maintaining client information on computers should also be done with caution to ensure the confidentiality of the client.

The purpose of record keeping is to provide records of customer progress and treatment continuity. The main goal is the well-being of the client.

Testing

It is legal for counselors to administer exams only if they have adequate training and guidance in the administration of certain tests. Counselors are also morally obligated to determine and clearly explain to clients the reason and objectives of the evaluation process. They should discuss the cultural bias of the tools and known limitations. A related problem concerns the use of test data - who receives this data and how it will be used. Without the clear oral consent of the client, the matter should not be discussed with anyone. This is necessary to ensure the trust and communication of the advisor's interest in the client's well-being.

Dual Role Relationships

Different roles include different ethical expectations, strengths, and responsibilities. There may be a conflict between these expectations if the mentor participates in any role other than that of a trained assistant. For example, building a social or sexual relationship with a counselor, being a student or counselor, or entering into a professional support relationship with a friend or family member.

Clear boundaries and environmental clarity and a supportive relationship process, will minimize possible abuse of power. Dual relationships have a high potential for client abuse, which is less powerful than counselors regardless of circumstances. If these power differences are not accepted and both parties agree to another type of relationship, the damage can be substantial.

Misrepresentation

Misrepresentation can occur when a counselor seeks directly or indirectly taking information, training, experience, and or expertise on a particular client type or problem. A professional code of ethics specifically requires counselors to acknowledge their limitations. They can work in such cases under surveillance/consultation with external specialists, refer to a specialist, or use joint therapy with a specialist.

Failure to consider other diagnostic and therapeutic approaches, such as physical examination, psychopharmacology, or testing is another matter of ethical ethics. For example, many clients experience stress that appears to be related to lower health conditions. A multidisciplinary approach is needed such as psychological and social change.

No code of conduct can cover all situations and situations. Moral issues involving the use of computers for testing and record keeping are now being addressed.

II

MEANING AND NATURE

Counseling psychology is a special psychological activity that facilitates personal performance and interaction with others throughout life by focusing on emotions, social, educational, educational, health-related, developmental, and organizational. Combining theory, research, practice, and sensitivity with multiculturalism, these specialties include many processes that help people improve their well-being, reduce stress and inequality, solve problems, and increase their ability to live longer. very active lives. Counseling psychology addresses both common growth issues and the problems associated with physical, emotional, and psychological disorders.

PURPOSES AND POSSIBILITY OF COUNSELLING

- Counseling psychology is a practical field of psychology. It is based on clear psychological principles or approaches. Counseling psychologists work with a variety of personal needs and problems that occur during one's lifetime. It includes family and marital affairs, sexual identity, bereavement, divorce and depression, fear, sexual harassment, retirement, etc.
- Some counselors specialize in groups or issues. People of all ages and backgrounds can benefit from this. All in all, a consultant psychologist works with a less disturbed client. Emphasis on their performance is

in well-being and self-esteem and reduces illness and malpractice. Counselors want to establish and develop relationships where clients will feel safe and comfortable exploring the issues they bring.

- As a therapist, the concern of counselors is to provide a therapeutic relationship that will support personal growth. Psychological assessment and clarification of client-counselor relationships. The skills of counseling psychologists are focused on developing and maintaining customer-counselor relationships. What matters is the ability to really listen to clients, to be able to empathize with their point of view, to hear their stories. Equally important is the ability to step back and evaluate, make decisions, interpret and view results.
- The counselors of psychologists should learn to deal with stress and emotions. In some cases, it may be appropriate to use the psychological test for which training is required and there are important management functions, especially the writing of customer reports. Good counseling ethics is nurtured by the counselor's reflection on performance and theoretical ideas and research. The counseling psychologist needs to know when to refer the client to another specialist, where the counseling relationship should end,
- and the ability to see the limitations of his or her job skills.
- The psychologists who counsel them perform so many different tasks that it is difficult to document all of them. A counseling psychologist can consult with various agencies (e.g., schools, government, NGOs), educate, conduct research, manage treatment, hold management positions, among others.
- Counselors learn and work in various fields. Some places where counseling professionals work and study are as follows:
- Vocational psychology
- Child development
- Adolescent development
- Adult development/aging
- Health psychology
- Mental illness
- Forensic psychology
- Sport psychology
- Neuropsychology
- Interpersonal relationships
- Assessment

- Rehabilitation
- Community psychology
- Crisis intervention
- Developmental disabilities
- Eating disorders
- Suicidal and homicidal tendencies
- Multiculturalism

CHARACTERISTICS OF EFFECTIVE COUNSELLING

Effective counseling is a two-way street. A collaborative effort is required by a counselor and counselor. It also requires a commitment to make sometimes difficult changes in behavior or patterns of thinking.

What the client expects to accomplish with the counselor should be clearly stated in the first paragraph of your counseling. The client and the consultant should discuss real-time scenarios to achieve goals and agree on how progress will be measured.

It is important that the client and the counselor build a good relationship where both feel comfortable, especially the client should feel comfortable with the mentor's personality, style, and style. An effective counselor can help point out obstacles in the way of a client's efforts to make changes in their lives. The counselor may suggest behavioral changes to help the client overcome obstacles. If these barriers include things beyond the control of the client, the consultant can teach coping strategies that will promote the well-being of clients in difficult situations.

An effective counselor can detect negative thoughts that may be feelings of sadness, depression, or anxiety. By encouraging the client to build on personal strengths and skills suggestions that can overcome the feelings of hopelessness they feel, a mentor can help that person develop a positive attitude.

A good counselor can help a client make positive changes in their relationships with others, helping them to identify behaviors that may contribute to a troubled relationship. Counselors can also teach effective ways of communicating, paving the way for honest communication with people in the life of a client who may be causing emotional pain.

The effectiveness of counseling may be determined when the client begins to receive information about his or her thoughts and behaviors that he or she may have previously avoided. Over time, they should be able to identify patterns in their performance, follow their sources and identify barriers to happiness and well-being. The result is personal growth that gives the client the power to control their own lives and enjoy good, life-affirming relationships with others.

APPLICATION OF COUNSELLING IN VARIOUS AREAS

A counselor can choose to specialize in various areas according to his or her interest and aptitude. Presented below are a few areas of application, among the many.

Relationship counseling

Relationship counseling is the process of counseling the parties of a relationship in order to try and reconcile differences. The relationship involved maybe people in a family, between employees in a workplace, or between a professional and a client. Relationship counselors are extremely helpful at any stage/type of a relationship. There are counselors specializing in premarital counseling as well as those working with married couples experiencing

difficulties of many years' duration. Relationship counseling aims to help recognize and better manage or reconcile troublesome differences and repeating patterns of distress. The goal of relationship counseling is to help couples improve communication skills, learn to handle conflicts constructively, and help to resolve old childhood issues that may be hindering the growth of a healthy relationship.

Rehabilitation counseling

Rehabilitation counseling aims to assist individuals with physical, mental, developmental, cognitive, and emotional disabilities to achieve their personal, career, and independent living goals in a systematic manner. The counseling process is like any other, involving communication, goal-setting, and initiating and augmenting beneficial growth or change through self-advocacy, psychological, vocational, social, and behavioral interventions.

The specific techniques and modalities utilized in the rehabilitation counseling process may include, but are not restricted to the following:

- Assessment and appraisal
- Diagnosis and treatment planning
- Career (vocational) planning; job analysis and job development
- Provide placement services, including assistance with reasonable accommodations
- Case management, referral, and service coordination
- Advocacy and interventions to remove environmental, employment, and attitudinal barriers
- Provision of consultation about and access to rehabilitation technology

Addiction Counselling

When an individual persists in the use of alcohol or other drugs despite problems related to the use of the substance, substance dependence may be diagnosed. Addiction is both a physiological and a psychosocial phenomenon. It can affect anyone from all walks of life. Counseling approaches generally integrate psychotherapeutically and coping skills-training techniques. The primary goal is to enhance and sustain patient motivation for change, establish and maintain abstinence from all psychoactive drugs, and foster the development of coping and problem-solving skills to thwart and ultimately eliminate impulses to —self-medicate‖ with psychoactive drugs.

Issues relevant to the mental and physical well-being of women

Rape is when one person wants and pursues a sexual act on, to, or inside another person who does not want to participate, and who does not fully and freely consent to take part in that act. Victims of rape can be severely traumatized by the assault and may have difficulty functioning as well as they had been used to prior to the assault, with disruption of concentration, sleeping patterns, and eating habits. It is common for the victim to experience Acute Stress Disorder, including symptoms similar to those of posttraumatic stress disorder, such as intense, sometimes unpredictable, emotions, and they may find it hard to deal with their memories of the event. It is important that the rape and assault survivors have a supportive network of family and friends along with professional help.

Counseling women may cover preventive aspects such as providing necessary education regarding the physical and psychological changes relating to puberty, pregnancy and menopause. It may involve educating family members also to provide necessary support at these phases of a women‘s life. Women may also require help in making career choices, improving their careers, and handling various difficulties at work.

Educational setting

A counselor can work in a school or college setting. Counselors are today vital members of the education team. They help students in the areas of academic achievement, personal/social development, and career development, ensuring today‘s students become the productive, well-adjusted adults of tomorrow. The counselor is required to possess the following skills: the ability to work with parents, students, faculty, college educational representatives, as well as community groups, understanding student maturity levels and the process of goal selection, ability to motivate students, and provide an academic incentive for success, ability to use culturally relevant and responsive strategies when planning programs and making presentations.

Career Counselling

Career counseling may include the provision of occupational information, modeling skills, written exercises, and exploration of career goals and plans. It also involves the use of personality or career interest assessments. When people seek out a career counselor or are referred to one, they may work with the counselor to evaluate skills, learn how to improve skills, learn how to successfully search for jobs, and develop methods for effectively applying and interviewing for work. The career counselor can also help individuals who have trouble maintaining jobs or who have certain skills that are no longer in demand. A career counselor can also be extremely helpful in situations where individuals need to change careers and at difficult times such as recession, downsizing, etc. The counselor assesses the clients‘ background, skills, and experience and helps identify other career options that may or may not have occurred to the displaced employee.

Counseling the aged

Old age brings about changes in lifestyles, activities, and relationships. Older people need to be counseled to utilize their earlier skills/ training etc. to stay connected with people. The problems of the elderly generally arise from three sources: Medical, Financial and Social. As people age, health-related problems are likely to occur. Vision and mobility are the two most threatening of them. It is important to counsel them, to stay healthy by adopting lifestyles that involve diet control, exercise regimen, and stress-free living.

The elderly may cope with aging through the following ways:

1. Plan and prepare from early years, particularly middle-age
2. Enhance and manage finances well. Focus on savings and investments
3. Pay attention to health.
4. Develop hobbies and sustain interpersonal interactions to the extent possible
5. Orient positively towards the personal concerns of grown-up children and their family

DIVERSITY IN COUNSELLING

Varying in a counseling relationship is a two-way street. As a consultant, you bring your legacy with you into your work, so you need to see how cultural contexts influence the guidelines you take with your clients.

Unless it takes into account the social and cultural context of clients and advisers, it is difficult to inform the nature of the clients‘ struggles. Student counseling often adheres to values — such as self-determination, expressiveness, openness and self-expression, and the struggle for independence — which differ from the values of clients from different cultural backgrounds. It is important for counselors to know how clients from different cultures can treat them as therapists, and how clients can recognize the importance of legal help. It is the responsibility of counselors to determine whether the consideration they have given for the condition and the effectiveness of the treatment is appropriate for culturally diverse clients.

Clearly, effective counseling should take into account the cultural impact on the client's performance, including the client's level of growth. Culture, values, and behaviors are shared by a group of individuals. Culture means more than just national or ethnic values; culture includes factors such as age, gender, religion, sexual orientation, physical and mental strength, and socioeconomic status.

ATTITUDE OF A PROFESSIONAL COUNSELLOR

Every mentor should make sure that everyone is important, important, and different in order to relate to them in a constructive and constructive way. This should sound like an experience and not an intangible philosophical concept. The mentor should have a genuine interest in the client and respect the mentor as an important, important, and important person. This is what Carl Rogers calls — unconditional good looks‖.

The counselor must believe that clients can make the change. The mentor should be optimistic. The belief that all counselors can, at least to a degree, change their moods, attitudes, moods, and behavior is crucial.

The mentor should see the mentor as an individual and a member of the community. The unique ways of a person and his performance in the outside world should be understood very carefully by counselors.

Counseling should not only be seen as a pain reliever but also as a way to improve growth and prevent pain.

The counselor should be prepared to devote time and energy to assisting the counselor. The mentor's dedication can easily have an impact on the client when he or she sees that the mentor demonstrates a deep commitment to getting involved in the lives of clients.

Counselors need to have a good knowledge of them. They must be aware of their feelings, thoughts, and behaviors and must understand and evaluate their attitudes, values, and motives for working with others, and they should always seek personal growth. Counselors with a positive sense of confidence, satisfaction, and self-discipline transcend their boundaries and are free to provide the necessary care to their clients and focus on ways to help them. These counselors are warm, understanding, honest, and have a general interest in the life of a counselor.

PERSONALITY OF EFFECTIVE COUNSELLORS

Though this list is not exhaustive and may seem too idealistic, effective counselors, by and large, tend to display the following personality traits and are continuously developing these traits: Effective counselors:

- *Have an identity.* They know who they are, what they are capableof becoming, what they want out of life, and what is essential.

- *Respect and appreciate themselves.* They can give and receivehelp and love out of their own sense of self-worth and strength. They feel adequate with others and allow others to feel powerful with them.

- *Are open to change.* They exhibit a willingness and courage toleave the security of the known if they are not satisfied with the way they are. They make decisions about how they would like to change, and they work toward becoming the person they want to become.

- *Make choices that are life-oriented.* They are aware of earlydecisions they made about themselves, others, and the world. They are not the victims of these early decisions, and they are willing to revise them if necessary. They are committed to living fully rather than settling for existence.

- *Are authentic, sincere, and honest.* They do not hide behindmasks, defenses, sterile roles, or facades.

- *Have a sense of humor.* They are able to put the events of life inperspective. They have not forgotten how to laugh, especially at their own weaknesses and contradictions.

- *Make mistakes and are willing to admit them.* They do notdismiss their errors lightly, yet they do not choose to dwell on misery.

- *Generally, live in the present.* They are not fixed in the past or onthe future. They are able to experience and be present with others in the ―now.‖

- *Appreciate the influence of culture.* They are aware of the waysin which their own culture affects them, and they respect the diversity of values espoused by other cultures. They are also sensitive to the unique differences arising out of social class, race, sexual orientation, and gender.

- *Have a sincere interest in the welfare of others.* This concern isbased on respect, care, trust, and are valuing of others.

- *Possess effective interpersonal skills.* They are capable of enteringthe world of others without getting lost in this world, and they strive to create collaborative relationships with others. They do not present themselves as polished salespersons, yet they have the capacity to take another person's position and work together toward consensual goals.

- *Become deeply involved in their work and derive meaning from it.* They can accept the rewardsflowing from their work, yetthey are not slaves to their work.

- *Are passionate.* They have the courage to pursue their passions,and they are passionate about life and their work. *Effective therapists are able to maintain healthy boundaries.* Althoughthey strive to be fully present for their clients, they don't carry the problems of their clients around with them during leisure hours. They know how to say no, which enables them to maintain balance in their lives.

VALUES IN COUNSELLING

The extent to which counselors should enter into a medical relationship is controversial. Counselors are often taught not to express their values. Yet they are not in the middle, and they have no value. Therapeutic interventions depend on basic values, and even the choice of words they use reflects their value system. It is neither possible nor desirable for counselors to be neutral in regard to the standards of the counseling relationship. Although the principles of counselors influence the way they act, it is possible to maintain a positive attitude.

Counselors need to be alert to the tendency to take on any of these two extremes. On the other hand there are advisers who have strong convictions and beliefs and who see it as their duty to influence customers to accept their standards. These counselors tend to guide their clients into 'positive attitudes and values.' On the other hand, counselors are adamant that they should avoid their own standards in their work and that the goal is to strive for effective counsel. . Because these counselors intend not to contact their clients, they are at risk of not being able to walk.

Studies have shown that counselor values influence all aspects of the treatment process, including diagnostic strategies, treatment objectives, identification of client problems to focus on treatment, selection of strategies, and evaluation of treatment outcomes. Clients are influenced by the prices of therapists and often take some of these values.

The role of the counselor is to create an environment in which clients can evaluate their thoughts, feelings, and actions and finally find the solutions that best suit them. The role of counselors is to help individuals find answers that are most in line with their values. Therefore, it is important for them to be aware of the nature of their principles and how their beliefs and standards apply to the interventions used in their professional work. The role of the Counselor is not to convince clients of the right course to take but to help them evaluate their behavior so that they can determine the quality of their service. If clients admit that they are not getting what they want, it is worthwhile to help them develop new ways of thinking and behaving to help them get closer to their goals. This is done with full respect for their right to decide what values they will use as a framework for life. People who seek advice are the ones who must articulate their values and principles, make informed decisions, choose a course of action, and take responsibility for their actions.

ETHICAL CONSIDERATIONS FOR A COUNSELLOR

Behavioral professional codes serve a number of purposes. They educate counselors and the general public about the responsibilities of the profession. They provide a basis for accountability, and through their coercion, clients are protected from unethical practices. Perhaps most importantly, ethical codes can provide a basis for thinking and improving your performance.

Code of conduct is often misrepresented, such as a list of rules and prohibitions that lead to punishment and wrongdoing if employees do not follow through. A compulsory Code of Conduct is an ethical code of ethics relating to a low level of professionalism, while enthusiastic ethics is a high standard of ethics that deals with doing what is best for clients. Moral values are more than just a list of things to avoid for fear of being punished. Behavior is a way of thinking about being the best job you can be. Good behavior is the approach taken by doctors who want to do their best for clients rather than simply meeting the lowest standards so as not to get into trouble.

Knowing and following a professional code of conduct is part of being an ethics expert, but these codes do not make advisory decisions. Interpreting professional ethics guidelines and applying them to specific situations requires greater sensitivity to ethics. Even responsible employees differ in their approach to applying ethical principles in certain situations. In your professional career, you will be challenged to deal with questions that always have obvious answers. You will need to take responsibility for deciding how to proceed in ways that will further the interests of your customers.

Putting Customer Needs Prior to Yours

As consultants, we cannot always keep our personal needs completely different from our relationships with clients. In terms of ethics, it is important that we know our needs and sees how such things can interfere with serving our customers effectively and ethically. Our working relationships with our customers are there for their benefit. The most important question you should always ask yourself is: — Whose needs do they meet in this relationship, my client's or mine? ‖ It requires a deep professional maturity to honestly assess how your behavior is affecting your clients. It is not uncommon for ethics to meet our personal needs through our professional work, but it is important that these needs are kept in perspective. A behavioral problem arises when we meet our needs, either in public or in private, at the expense of our clients' needs. It is important that we avoid exploiting or harming clients.

Right of Informed Permit

Regardless of the framework of the counselors' theory, informed consent is a requirement of ethical and legal principles that are an integral part of the treatment process. It also establishes the basic foundation for creating a working alliance and collaborative relationship between client and therapist. Informed consent includes the right of clients to be informed of their treatment and to make independent decisions about it. Providing clients with the information they need to make informed decisions often promotes effective client cooperation in their counseling process. By educating your customers about their rights and obligations, you are empowering both of them and building a trusting relationship with them.

Confidentiality

Confidentiality and special communication are two related but not identical ideas. Both of these ideas are based on the client's right to privacy. Confidentiality is a moral concept, and in many states, it is the legal duty of physicians not to disclose information about a client. Specialized communication is a legal term that usually prevents the disclosure of confidential communications in a trial.

Confidentiality is important in developing a trustworthy and productive relationship with the client - and the therapist. Because no real cure is possible unless clients rely on the confidentiality of their revelations from their therapists, professionals have a responsibility to explain the level of confidentiality that can be promised. Counselors have a legal obligation to discuss the nature and purpose of confidentiality with their clients prior to the counseling process. In addition, clients have the right to know that their therapist may be discussing certain relationship details with a manager or colleague.

Although most advisers agree on the value of confidentiality, they recognize that it cannot be considered complete. There are times when confidential information should be disclosed, and there are many instances where maintaining or violating privacy becomes a vague issue. In deciding when to maintain confidentiality, clinicians should consider the legal requirements, the institution in which they work, and the client they work for. Because these situations are often not clearly defined by the accepted codes of conduct, counselors should use professional judgment.

There is a legal requirement to break confidentiality in cases involving child abuse, abuse of the elderly, abuse of dependent adults, and danger to self or others. All mental health practitioners and interns need to be aware of their duty to report in these situations and to know the limitations of confidentiality. Here are some other circumstances in which information must legally be reported by counselors:

- When the therapist believes a client under the age of 16 is the victim of incest, rape, child abuse, or some other crime
- When the therapist determines that the client needs hospitalization
- When information is made an issue in a court action

In general, the counselor‘s primary obligation is to protect client disclosures as a vital part of the therapeutic relationship. Informing clients about the limits of confidentiality does not necessarily inhibit successful counseling.

Ethical Dilemmas in Assessment and Diagnosis

Diagnosis and diagnosis are entirely related to the practice of counseling and psychotherapy, and both are often regarded as important in the planning of treatment. Regardless of their theoretical position, clinicians need to participate in testing, which is often an ongoing part of the treatment process. The evaluation should not precede and determine the intervention; rather, it is woven in and out of the healing process as an integral part of the treatment itself. This test may be subject to review as the physician collects additional data during the treatment session. Some physicians view screening as part of the process leading to a formal diagnosis.

Evaluation involves assessing the relevant aspects of the client's life in order to identify themes in order to further evaluate the counseling process. Diagnosis, sometimes part of the diagnostic process, involves identifying specific psychiatric disorders based on the pattern of symptoms that lead to a specific diagnosis. Both diagnosis and diagnosis can be understood as providing guidance on the treatment process.

Psychodiagnosis analysis and interpretation of client problems. It may include a description of the causes of the client's difficulty, an account of how these problems started overtime, the classification of any disorders, the specification of the preferred treatment procedure, and the degree of probability of successful treatment. The purpose of the diagnosis in counseling and psychotherapy is to identify the disorder in the current behavior and health of the client. Once the problem areas have been clearly identified, the counselor and client are able to establish treatment policy objectives, and the treatment plan can be tailored to the client's unique needs.

Most staff members view screening and diagnosis as a continuous process focused on understanding the client. A participatory vision involving the client as an active participant in the treatment process suggests that both the therapist and the client are busy with the search and finding process from the first to the last session.

Ethical issues may be created when the diagnosis is made with strong intentions without the help of a specialist, which often involves giving the client improperly in the diagnostic phase. However, it is the clinical, legal, and ethical obligation of clinicians to diagnose clients with life-threatening complications such as environmental disorders, schizophrenia, bipolar disorder, and suicidal ideation.

It is important to examine everyone, which includes assessing the size of the mind, body, and spirit. Therapists need to consider biological processes as much as possible the underlying features of psychological symptoms and work closely with physicians. Client prices can be helpful resources in finding solutions to their problems, and spiritual and religious values often illuminate customer concerns.

Dual and Multiple Relationships in Counseling Practice

Two or more relationships, whether sexual or non-sexual, occur when counselors take on two (or more) roles simultaneously or respectively with a client. This may involve taking on more than one professional role or combining professional and non-professional roles.

Many types of non-professional relationships or multiple non-sexual relationships pose a challenge to employees. Other examples of non-bisexual relationships include the roles of teacher and therapist or manager and therapist; trade in goods or medical services; borrowing money from a client; providing treatment for a friend, co-worker, or relative; engaging in community-client relations; receiving an expensive gift from a client; or getting into business with a customer. Many other relationships are openly abusive and severely hurt the client and the professional. For example, emotional or sexual involvement with the current client is clearly not ethical, professional, and illegal. Engaging in premarital sex is unwise, can be abusive, and is often viewed as inappropriate.

Because bisexual and multidimensional relationships are complex and multidimensional, there are a few simple and complete solutions to solve them. It is not always possible to play a single role in your work as a mentor, and it is not always desirable. You may have to deal with managing multiple roles, no matter what your working environment or the number of clients you work for. Contemplate this notion as you interact with other people before engaging in questionable conduct. Ethical and judicial thinking begins when codes of conduct are used in certain contexts. The revised ACA Code of Ethics (ACA, 2005) emphasizes that counseling professionals must learn to manage multiple roles and responsibilities in an ethical manner. These include dealing effectively with the power disparities found in counseling and training relationships, balancing border issues, dealing with non-professional relationships, and striving to avoid using force in ways that could cause harm to clients, students, or supervisors.

Although two or more relationships carry environmental risks, it is a mistake to conclude that these relationships remain immoral and lead to harm and exploitation. Some of these relationships can be beneficial to customers if used responsibly and honestly.

Ways of minimizing risk

The following guidelines may be helpful in ensuring minimal risk:

- Set healthy boundaries early in the therapeutic relationship. Informed consent is essential from the beginning and throughout the therapy process.

- Involve clients in ongoing discussions and in the decision-making process, and document your discussions. Discuss with your clients what you expect of them and what they can expect of you.

- Consult with fellow professionals as a way to maintain objectivity and identify unanticipated difficulties. Realize that you don‘t need to make a decision alone.

- When dual relationships are potentially problematic, or when the risk for harm is high, it is always wise to work under supervision. Document the nature of this supervision and any actions you take in your records.

- Self-monitoring is critical throughout the process. Ask yourself whose needs are being met and examine your motivations for considering becoming involved in a dual or multiple relationships.

CHARACTERISTICS OF A SUCCESSFUL COUNSELLEE

A large part of the positive effect of counseling is determined by the counselor. The level of pathology of the counselor, the motivation for change, the expectation of treatment, coping skills, personal history, and other external resources all influence how the counseling experience will work. Counselors clearly benefit by actively participating in the counseling process. When counselors are highly cooperative, motivated, and engaged, they are often involved, leading to effective counseling. The characteristics of the counselor, such as the attitude of seeking help and the style of attachment were found to be related to the use of the counselor for counseling, as well as expectations and outcome. Discrimination against mental illness can make people less aware of problems and seek help. Avoidance counselors have been shown to face greater risks and fewer benefits, and are less likely to seek professional help, compared to highly protected counselors. Educating counselors about what to expect from counseling can improve counseling satisfaction, duration of treatment and outcomes.

The counselee characteristics that strongly influence counseling include the following:

- The kind/nature of problem
- The scope of the problem
- The historical and idiosyncratic pattern employed to solve problems and resolve issues

- Demographic characteristics such as socioeconomic status, gender and developmental level
- Personality characteristics
- Intelligence
- Reading ability
- Cognitive style
- Temperament
- Level of motivation
- Counselee‘s degree of functioning
- Strengths and resources of the counselee
- Reluctance and resistance
- Values and beliefs of the counselee
- Cultural background and experiences

Successful counselee will display the following characteristics:

- Openness to new experiences, willing to do something new or different
- Responsive, willing to listen to other people, to accept negative as well as positive feedback, to take instructions, and to do what is expected
- Assertive, willing to ask for help, clarification, or additional instruction or guidance
- communicates expectations clearly
- Understands the process of counseling and allows a reasonable amount of time for progress
- Goal-oriented, focused on producing results or changes
- Enthusiastic, eager to learn
- Attending sessions regularly and being on time
- Working diligently on all the homework that they might be required to do

- Knowing that they are responsible for their own success

COUNSELLEE EXPECTATIONS

Counselors bring expectations and beliefs into counseling situations. These expectations can affect both the counseling process and its outcome. Counselor expectations affect many aspects of counseling, including the length of their stay in counseling, their satisfaction with counseling, and how quickly and quickly they progress. The expectations of counselors should be considered and considered in order to improve the effectiveness of counseling.

The strongest expectation of a counselor is to find someone who is knowledgeable, honest, professional, and acceptable counselor who can be trusted. The mentor is expected to have a warm interest in each mentor, highly trained and experienced,

and confidence in his ability to assist a counselor. The counselor is expected to focus on the problem at the individual level, prepare well for each interview, be comfortable with the counselor and his or her individual problem and maintain confidentiality.

Counseling psychology is a special psychological activity that facilitates personal performance and interaction with others throughout life by focusing on emotions, social, educational, educational, health-related, developmental, and organizational. Combining theory, research, practice, and sensitivity with multiculturalism, these specialties include many processes that help people improve their well-being, reduce stress and inequality, solve problems, and increase their ability to live longer. very active lives. Counseling psychology addresses both common growth issues and the problems associated with physical, emotional, and psychological disorders.

III

PSYCHOANALYTIC THEORY AND TECHNIQUES

Different approaches to counselling are based on the varying conceptions of human personality structure and dynamics and are subject to the limitations to which the personality theories are prone. The term approach' is used in preference to theory' as no single theory has yet been able to encompass all the aspects of counselling.

Freud's psychoanalytic system is a model of personality development, a philosophy of human nature and a method of psychotherapy. He focused on the psychodynamic factors that motivate the motivated behaviour, on the role of the unconscious and developed the first therapeutic procedures for understanding and modifying the structure of one's basic character.

VIEW OF HUMAN NATURE:

The Freudian view of human nature is basically deterministic. According to Freud, people's behaviour is determined by irrational forces, unconscious motivations, biological and instinctual drives and certain psychosexual stages during the first six years of life.

Instincts are central to the Freudian approach. Freud originally used the term —*libido*" to refer to sexual energy; later broadened it to include the energy of all the life instincts. He included all pleasurable acts in his concepts of life instincts; he saw the goal of life as gaining pleasure and avoiding pain.

Freud also postulated the concept —*death instincts" (Thanatos),* which accounted for the *aggressive* drive. At times, he asserted, people manifest through their behaviour an unconscious wish to die or hurt themselves or others. In his view, both sexual and aggressive drives are powerful determinants of why people act as they do.

STRUCTURE OF PERSONALITY:

According to the psychoanalytic view, personality consists of three systems; the id, the ego, and the superego. However, one's personality should be understood as functioning as a whole rather than three discrete segments. According to Freudian view, the dynamics of personality consists of the ways in which psychic energy is distributed to the id, ego and superego.

The Id

The Id is the biological component and the original system of personality. The Id is the primary source of psychic energy and the seat of the instincts. It lacks organizations, and it is blind, demanding and insistent. The Id cannot tolerate tension and it functions to discharge tension immediately and return to a homeostatic condition. Ruled by the pleasure principle, which is aimed at reducing tension, avoiding pain and gaining pleasure, the Id is illogical, amoral and driven by one consideration; to satisfy instinctual need in accordance with the pleasure principle. The Id never matures but remains the spoiled brat of personality. It does not think but only wishes or acts. The Id is largely unconscious, or out of awareness

The Ego

The Ego has contact with the external world of reality. It is the _executive' that governs, controls and regulates the personality. It mediates between the instincts and the surrounding environment. The ego controls the consciousness and exercise censorship. Ruled by the reality principle, Ego does realistic and logical thinking and formulates plans of actions for satisfying needs. While the Id knows only subjective reality, the Ego distinguishes between mental images and the things in the external world.

The Superego

The Superego is the judicial branch of personality. It is a person's moral code, the main concern being whether action is good or bad, right or wrong. It represents the ideal rather than a real and strives not for pleasure but for perfection. It represents the traditional values and ideals of society. It functions to inhibit the id impulses, persuade the ego to substitute moralistic goals for realistic ones and to strive for perfection. The superego, as the internalization of the standards of parents and society, is related to psychological rewards (feelings of pride and self-love) and punishments (guilt and inferiority)

CONSCIOUSNESS AND THE UNCONSCIOUSNESS:

For Freud, consciousness is a thin slice of the total mind. Like the greater part of the iceberg that lies below the surface of the water, the larger part of the mind exists below the surface of awareness. The unconsciousness stores up all experiences, memories and repressed material. Needs and motivations that are out of awareness are also outside the sphere of conscious control. Most psychological functioning exists in the out-of-awareness realm. The aim of psychoanalytic therapy, therefore, is to make the unconscious process, the roots of all forms of neurotic symptoms and behaviours.

ANXIETY:

The concept of anxiety is also essential to the psychoanalytic approach. Anxiety is a state of tension that motivates us to do something. It develops out of a conflict among the id, ego and superego over control of the available psychic energy. Its function is to warn of impending danger.

There are three kinds of anxiety; the reality, neurotic and moral. Reality anxiety is the fear of danger from the external world, and the level of such anxiety is proportionate to the degree of real threat. Neurotic anxiety is the fear that the instincts will get out of hand and cause to do something for which one will be punished. Moral anxiety is the fear of one's own conscience.

EGO-DEFENSE MECHANISMS

When the ego cannot control anxiety by rational and direct methods, it relies on unrealistic ones-Ego-defense mechanisms. Ego-defence mechanisms help the individual cope with anxiety and prevent the ego from being overwhelmed. They can have adaptive value if they do not become a style of life to void facing reality. Defence mechanisms have two characteristics in common; they either deny or distort reality and they operate on an unconscious level. Some common Ego defences are;

- Repression – It is a means of defence through which threatening or painful thoughts are excluded from awareness. It is an involuntary removal of something from consciousness.

- Denial – Denial is a way of distorting what the individual thinks, feels or perceives in a traumatic situation. It generally operates at preconscious and conscious levels. It consists of defending against anxiety, expressing the opposite impulse.

- Reaction formation – defending against a threatening impulse by actively expressing the opposite impulse.

- Displacement – Discharging impulses by shifting from a threatening object to a _safer target'

- Rationalization – this involves explaining the failures or losses. It helps to justify specific behaviours and it aids in coping with disappointments.

- Sublimation – This involves diverting sexual energy into other channels, ones that are usually socially acceptable and sometimes even admirable.

- Regression – Reverting to a form of behaviours that they have outgrown.

- Introjection – This mechanism consists of taking in and _swallowing' the values and standards of others.

- Identification – Although this is a part of the development process by which children learn sex-role behaviours, it can also be a defensive reaction.

- Compensation – This consists of masking perceived weakness or developing certain positive aspects (skills, attributes, etc)to make up for limitations.

- Ritual and undoing – At times people perform elaborate rituals as a way of undoing acts for which they feel guilty.

DEVELOPMENT OF PERSONALITY

- According to the Freudian psychoanalytic view, the three areas of personal and social development – love and trust, dealing with negative feelings and developing a positive acceptance of sexuality are all grounded from the first six years of life. This period is the foundation on which later personality development is built.

- **The first year of life: the oral stage** –Two activities are developedduring this developmental period- the oral-incorporative behaviour and oral aggressive behaviour are considered to be the prototypes of some of the character traits of adulthood.

- Oral incorporative behaviour involves pleasurable stimulation of the mouth. Adults who exhibit excessive oral needs (such as excessive eating, chewing, talking, smoking and drinking) may have an *oral fixation.* Deprivation of oral gratification during infancy is assumed tolead to problems in adulthood.

- The oral-aggressive period begins when the infant teethes. Adult characteristics such as sarcasm, hostility, aggression, gossip, and making _biting‘ comments are related to events of this development period.

- Later personality problems that stem from the oral stage are the development of a view about the world based on mistrust, fear of reaching out to others, rejection of affection, fear of loving and trusting, low self-esteem, isolation and withdrawal and inability to form or maintain intense relationships.

- **Ages 1-3: The anal stage** - The tasks to be mastered in this stage ofdevelopment are learning independence, personal power and autonomy and learning how to recognize and deal with negative feelings. When toilet training begins during the second year, children have their first major experience with discipline. The method of toilet training and the parents' feeling attitudes and reactions toward the child can have far-reaching effects on the formation of reactions toward the child can have far-reaching effects on the formation of personality traits, Later personality problems. In contrast, other parents might focus too much attention on their children during this stage.

If strict toilet – training methods are used, children may express their anger by expelling their faces at inappropriate places and times. This behaviour can lay the foundation for adult characteristics such as cruelty, inappropriate displays of anger and extreme disorderliness

Freud described this as *anal aggressive* personality. In contrast, other parents might focus too much attention on their children's bowel movements by giving praise whenever they defecate, which can contribute to a child's exaggerated view of the importance of this activity. This focus might be associated with a person's need for being productive.

- **Ages 3-6: The phallic stage –** In this period there is increased motorand perceptual development as well as interpersonal skills. Sexual activity becomes more intense and now the focus of attention is on the genitals – the boy's penis and the girl's clitoris.

- According to the orthodox Freudian view, the basic conflict of the phallic stage, centres on the unconscious desires that children develop for the parent of the opposite sex. Because these feelings are of such a threatening nature, they are typically repressed; yet powerful determinants of lateral sexual development and adjustment. Long with this comes the unconscious wish of the child to _do away with' the competition – the parent of the same sex.

- In the *male phallic stage,* the boy craves the attention of his mother, feels antagonistic toward his father and is known as the *Oedipus complex.* At this time the boy typically develops specific fears relatedto his penis. *Castration anxiety* plays a central role in the boy's life at this time. He fears that his father will retaliate by cutting off his offending organ. If the oedipal conflict is properly resolved, the boy replaces his sexual longings for his mother with more acceptable forms of affection. He develops strong identification with his father through which he experiences various satisfaction. He becomes more like his father and may adopt many of his father's mannerisms.

- The Electra complex is the girl's counterpart to the Oedipus complex.

The girl is said to develop negative feelings toward her mother when she discovers the absence of a penis, the condition known as *penis envy.* The girl later on like a boy begins the identification process by takingon some of the characteristics of her mother's behaviour.

- **Ages 6-12: The latency stage** –This is the period of relative rest. Themajor structures of personality are largely formed, as are the relationships between these subsystems. New interests replace infantile sexual impulses. Socialization takes place and children direct their interests to the larger world. The sexual drive is sublimated, to some extent, to activities in school, hobbies, sports and friendships and with members of the same sex.

- A major characteristic of oral, anal and phallic stages is a *narcissistic* orientation or an inward and self-centred preoccupation. During the middle-childhood years, there is a turning relationship with others. This period prevails until the onset of puberty.

Age 12-18: The genital stage –Young adults move into the genitalstage unless they become fixated at an earlier period of psychosexual development. Old themes of phallic stages are revived. Adolescents typically develop an interest in the opposite sex, engage in some sexual experimentation and begin to assume adult responsibilities. There is a trend away from narcissism and toward altruistic behaviour and concern for others. They develop intimate relationships, become free of parental influence, and develop the capacity to be interested in others. Freud was primarily concerned with the impact of resolving sexual issues during the first six years of life. He did not go into great detail in discussing the crises associated with adolescence or the stages of adulthood.

JUNG'S PERSPECTIVES ON THE DEVELOPMENT OF PERSONALITY

Carl Jung focused on the role of purpose in human development, presenting a more creative, optimistic view of humankind. He believed that a person had more energy than that derived from sexual drives and that one was always developing towards the wholeness and self-fulfilment (Individuation), using energy to be —creatively purposeful‖ and searching for a balance among body, mind and spirit.

Jung believed that the —transcendent function‖ (use of the energy to integrate and transcend conflict) mediates the relation between the conscious and the unconscious. He differentiated between the personal unconscious (painful, threatening experiences repressed or ignored) and the collective unconscious (buried memories based on the wisdom of the ancestral past). This differentiation helps in understanding and interpreting unconscious material – that is symbols. Through his construct of collective unconscious, Jung paid more attention than did Freud to the role of culture in the development of the human personality. In time of war, for example, one can imagine the forces of collective unconscious, causing people to unite in aggression.

Other major Jungian concepts include the persona (public mask or social façade one displays in various situations), the animus (masculine side), the anima (feminine side), extroversion (orientation toward the outer, objective world), and introversion (orientation toward the inner, subjective world). These concepts led to Jung's postulation of four types of people: thinking, feeling, sensing, and intuiting. In distinguishing among these psychological types, Jung pointed out that persons with different types communicate with great difficulty. For example, an intuitive person will be impatient with the practical approach of the sensation-oriented person. The thinking type will have trouble with the feeling type and vice-versa. All these types, in varying degrees of extroversion and introversion, exist within every human;

however, one type tends to be more pronounced than the others.

Jung was not as deterministic as Freud. He postulated spiritual development throughout adult life, focusing particularly on one‘s capacity in midlife to integrate unconscious and conscious aspects of personality in order to become an authentic, spiritual individual.

IV

MODERN-DAY TRENDS

Modern trends in cognitive thinking contribute to the realization that our current behavior in the world is a repetition of patterns set during one of the first stages of development. Relationship theory helps us to see the ways in which clients interact with other important people in the past and how they promote these early experiences in current relationships. For many medical clients who have problems such as separation and separation, intimacy, dependence compared to independence, and identity, these new conditions can provide a framework for understanding how and where features of expansion have been obsessed. This chapter elaborates on these perspectives and discusses the techniques used by the psychoanalytic approach.

SELF PSYCHOLOGY AND RELATIONSHIP WITH THE PURPOSE

Modern psychoanalytic thinkers (primarily Melanie Klein, Ronald Fairbairn, Donald W. Winnicott, Harry Guntrip, Margaret Mahler, Heinz Kohut, and Otto Kernberg) emphasize ego and relationships. humans rather than the id and biological drives they are born with as the basis for human development. The main motivation of a person from birth is considered to be communication and relationships, as opposed to the release of pressure from sexual impulses and aggression. It focuses on the relationship between a person and a real person, between a person and his or her mental image or representation of real people, and between images of a person or presentations from important past relationships with real people.

Significant personality development begins in the pre-editorial phase, with the child's relationship with the primary caregiver, usually the mother, rather than with the child's relationship with the father during the Freudian oedipal. The mother becomes the first thing in the baby's love. In the early stages of infancy, when a baby is unable to isolate itself, the baby's ability to self-identify to develop a sense of security within itself and the environment depends on the mother's sensitivity to her baby and her ability to empathize and empathize. enlarge. If the needs of the baby are not met by the symbiotic stage, the baby's ego divides, retreats, and hides to avoid the anxiety caused by the non-participation of essential needs on an ongoing basis. The ego divides into what Winnicott (1965) calls the true man and the false man. True identity is at the core of human life and is able to relate to others. False identity appears to be a protection against malnutrition, and insecurity. Hiding in a foreign country and relationships. Thus, failure or failure in early maternal upbringing leads to false behavior and prevents the development of the whole ego. Anger is seen by these theoretical students as a reaction or reaction to a frustrating relationship rather than a natural feeling.

The ego goes through many stages of positions between the infant and the young child, forming symbiotic relationships with the mother to stages of separation and separation. The infant's self-esteem and severity in early relationships form the development of self-esteem, which includes the potential for love and relationships. Separation and Sight, the defenses a person uses due to the wrong relationship of the substance, interfere with healthy ego growth and can contribute to pathologies such as narcissistic character disorder, borderline states, and psychiatry.

TREATMENT PROCEDURE

1 Objective of Treatment

The two goals of Freudian psychoanalytic therapy are to make the person faint and strengthen the ego so that the behavior is more based on reality and the study of natural longing. The successful analysis is believed to lead to significant changes in the personality and structure of the character. Childhood experiences are rebuilt, discussed, interpreted, and analyzed. The process is not only about solving problems and learning new behaviors but also digging deeper into the past and improving the level of self-awareness that is thought to be needed in order to change character.

2 Duties and responsibilities of the therapist

In classical psychoanalysis, the therapist reveals very little and maintains a sense of neutrality in an effort to promote transfer relationships, in which their clients will make assumptions for themselves. These predictions, which have their origins in unfinished and repressed cases and their analysis, are considered the essence of clinical practice.

Although the client recovers and shows classic 'emotional' symptoms during the session, referral neurosis is not intended to disrupt the client's performance outside of the analysis hour. When a client's emotional transmission leads to negative behavior outside of the session, it is called 'outside play'. Important imitation is viewed as harmful.

The primary function of the analysis is to assist the client in acquiring self-awareness, honesty, and effective personal relationships in dealing with concerns in a practical way, as well as in managing unexpected and irrational behavior. Collaborative relationships are first established between the therapist by listening and interpreting extensively. It focuses heavily on client arguments and the therapist decides to make appropriate explanations. The main task of translation is to speed up the process of unconscious objects. The analyst listens to the gaps and inconsistencies of the client's story. It conveys the meaning of reported dreams and free association, scrutinizes during the treatment session, and is always sensitive to clues about the client's feelings about the analyst. The analyst also teaches clients the meaning of treatment procedures so that they can gain an understanding of the problems, increase their awareness of alternatives and thus gain more rational control over lives.

3 EVENTS AND KALITE AND RELATIONSHIP RELATIONSHIPS

Classical psychoanalysis is a deep and long-term process. Free consultation, client reporting on their feelings, experiences, organizations, memories, and dreams to the analyst without any research on the ‖coremons‖ of the process. However, in practice-focused mindfulness, although all these methods can be followed by the therapist remains alert to the manifestations of transmission and working with dreams and unconscious objects. Treatment sessions are cut short once clients have clarified and accepted their emotional problems, understand the roots of their traumatic history, and may combine their awareness of patent problems with their current relationships.

The client's relationship with the analyst is considered through the transfer process, which is the essence of the psychological analysis process. A referral is an exchange of ignorance in a commentator made by a client of emotions and dreams, both positive and negative. If the treatment is going to produce a change, negative, which is a shift in response to an important one, something in the client's past. If treatment is to produce a change, a referral relationship should be worked out, by examining unconscious assets and self-defense. The therapist in this process is closely involved in unresolved conflicts within the therapist. Counter-transfer becomes an inevitable part of a medical relationship. It refers to the irrational response physicians have to clients that may affect their perception.

The client-therapeutic relationship is very important in psychoanalytic theory, especially in the functioning of the referral state, where clients receive information from their unconscious psychodynamics. This approach assumes that without this dynamic self-understanding there will be no major personal change or resolution of current conflicts.

STRATEGIES

1 KEEPING THE RENEWAL FRAMEWORK.

The psychoanalytic process emphasizes the maintenance of a specific framework intended to achieve the goals of this type of treatment. Maintaining an analytical framework refers to a whole range of process factors, such as analyst-related anonymity, consistency and consistency of meetings, and the start and end of sessions over time. One of the most powerful aspects of mind-altering therapy is that the dynamic framework itself is a therapeutic component, which compares the emotional level with normal infant nutrition. Analysts try to limit the movement of this fixed pattern (such as holidays, changes in payments, or changes in meeting place).

2 FREE ORGANIZATION

Free integration is a key component of psychotherapy, and it plays an important role in the process of maintaining an analysis framework. In a casual relationship, clients are encouraged to say whatever comes to mind, no matter how painful, stupid, small, irrational, or trivial. Clients flow with any feelings or thoughts by reporting them immediately without testing. As the analytical work progresses, more and more clients will occasionally move away from this basic rule, and these arguments will be interpreted by the therapist when it is time to do so.

Free association is one of the basic tools used to open the doors of unconscious desires, dreams, conflicts, and motives. This process often leads to some recollection of past experiences and, in some cases, the release of inhibited emotions (catharsis). This release is not considered important in itself, however. During the free assembly process, the therapist's job is to identify the compressed items that are unconscious. The sequence of organizations directs the consultant in understanding the communication clients make between events. Obstruction or disruption to integration serves as indicators of things that cause anxiety. The therapist translates things to clients, directing them to an increased understanding of basic dynamics.

As analysts listen to their clients' free organizations, they hear not only the above content but also the hidden meaning. Nothing the client says is taken from face value. For example, fluency may suggest that the emotions expressed are counterproductive. Areas that customers do not talk about are as important as the places they talk about.

3 DEFINITION

Interpretation involves the identification of the analyst, explaining and even teaching the client the meanings of the behaviors that appear in dreams, free association, contradictions, and therapeutic relationships themselves. The task of translation is to allow the ego to integrate something new and to speed up the process of revealing something more unconscious.

4 DREAM ANALYSIS

During sleep, self-defense declines, and feelings of depression arise, Freud sees dreams _like a royal road leading to the unconscious ngoba, in which the unconsciousness of the sufferer is expressed in a more subtle or symbolic way rather than directly revealed.

Dreams have two levels of content: hidden content and manifest content. Hidden content contains hidden, symbolic, and ignorant motives, desires, needs, and fears. Because they are so painful and frightening, unconscious sexuality and aggression that create subtle content are transformed into the most terrifying, dreamy reality as they appear in a dreamer. The process of subtle interpretation is called dreamwork. The therapist's job is to uncover hidden meanings by studying the symbols in the visual content of the dream. During the session, the therapist may ask the client to freely associate with a particular portion of the dream content for the purpose of revealing hidden meanings. Gradually, they are able to reveal the meaning of their dream.

5 ANALYSIS AND DESCRIPTION OF BIRTH

Resistance, a basic concept in the performance of psychological analysis, anything that works against medical progress and prevents the client from producing unconscious objects previously. In particular, resistance is the client's reluctance to bring over awareness of oppressed coma. Resistance means any thought, attitude, feeling, or action (consciousness or fainting) that is encouraging

the current situation also enters the path of change. During free association or dreaming, a client may have evidence of not wanting to associate certain thoughts, feelings, and information. Freud viewed resistance as a subtle variation that people use to prevent anxiety and the unbearable pain that can arise when they realize their emotions and feelings are suppressed.

As a protection against anxiety, resistance works especially in psychotherapy to prevent clients and therapists from succeeding in their concerted effort to gain insight into the dynamics of fainting. Because resistance prevents threatening objects from entering the awareness, analytical therapists point to it, and clients should deal with it if they hope to deal with the conflict in a practical way. The description of the therapists is intended to help clients know the reasons for the resistance so that they can deal with it. As a general rule, therapists identify and interpret the most obvious resistance in order to reduce the likelihood that clients will refuse to be interpreted and increase their chances of starting to look at their counter-behaviors.

Opposition is not just something to be overcome. Because they represent defenses that are common in everyday life, they need to be recognized as tools that prevent anxiety but interfere with the ability to accept change that can lead to more a satisfying life. It is very important for therapists to respect clients' opposition and help them work with their immune system. Properly managed, resistance can be one of the most important tools in understanding a client.

6 ASSESSMENT

Freudian's discovery that man is often motivated by thought and behavior by ignorance is crucial. Freud was probably the first psychologist to point out the importance of anxiety. He also had a hand in the therapist must have an attitude of misconduct.

The psychoanalytic process requires a lot of time, motivation and money. It is also criticized for one's preconceived notions, exposing them as evil desires that are suppressed. Emphasis is placed on the experience of childhood. This approach also minimizes the importance of status events. Properties shown may not be fully displayed or verified.

Proper use of psychoanalytic techniques requires more training than most therapists experience in their training program. Considering the initial client history is often helpful in understanding and working with the current client situation. Even if you may not agree with all the structures of the psychoanalytic past, you can still draw on many psychoanalytic ideas as a framework to understand your clients and help them gain a deeper understanding of the roots of their conflicts.

It is therefore clearly shown that modern psychoanalytic styles have important implications in many areas of human interaction such as intimate relationships, family and child rearing, and therapeutic relationships.

V

SLAB- II : (HYPOTHETICAL PERSPECTIVES) PHILANTHROPICAL THEORIES AND TECHNIQUES

In the 1960s and 1970s there was a growing interest among counselors in the "third court" in medicine as an alternative to psychological and behavioral analysis. Under this heading are available fall treatments, a personalized approach, and Gestalt therapy, all of which are experiences and relationships.

Generally, existence and personality, both emphasize values such as freedom, choice, values, personal responsibility, independence, purpose, and meaning. Both methods place little emphasis on the role of strategies in the treatment process, and instead emphasize the importance of real interactions. They differ in the fact that atheists take the position that we are concerned about choosing to create identity in a world that has no internal meaning. The Humanists, on the other hand, occupy a position that raises the slightest concern that each of us has natural forces that we can express and can find meaning in them.

PERSONAL VIEW

A person-centered approach is based on ideas from a human perspective, and can also be categorized as a branch of existing theory. In the early 1940s Rogers developed what came to be known as indirect counseling as a response to correction and psychoanalytic methods of individual therapy. His theory has emphasized the creation of an advisor for a climate that is conducive to climate change. Rogers has challenged the legitimacy of commonly accepted medical procedures such as counseling, counseling, persuasion, teaching, diagnosis, and translation. Inexperienced counselors avoid sharing too much with their clients, and instead focus more on demonstrating and clarifying customer communication verbally and non-verbally. Roger's basic assumption was that people deserve to be trusted, that they have great potential to understand and solve their problems without direct intervention on the part of the therapist, and that they are able to grow self-directed when engaging in a medical relationship. Attitudes and personal characteristics of the therapist and the quality of the client / therapeutic relationship are the main determinants of the outcome of the treatment process.

Rogers developed a systematic theory of humanity and applied this theory of self-reliance to the work of counseling individuals. His client-centered approach gradually expanded its influence in various fields far from its origins. Because of Roger's ever-growing influence, including his interest in how people acquire, manage, share, or delegate power and control over others and themselves, his view has become known as a personalized approach.

VIEW OF HUMAN NATURE

The consistent theme is full of all Rogers‘ writings and works. This theme is a profound belief in human tendency to grow in an unloving and constructive way when a climate of respect and trust is established. He strongly believed that humans were intelligent, capable, self-sufficient, and capable of leading productive, productive lives, emphasizing that there were three therapeutic qualities that fostered a climate that fostered growth where people could move forward and become what they were. of being.

These qualities are (1) consistency (integrity, or authenticity), (2) unconditional positive (acceptance and care), and (3) accurate understanding of empathy (the ability to deeply understand another person's independent world). According to Rogers, if these attitudes are conveyed by the facilitator, those assisted will be less self-reliant and more open to themselves and their world, and will behave in more social and constructive ways. The basic filling goal suggests that people move on to health care if the path seems open to them. Therefore, the purpose of counseling is to liberate clients and create those conditions that will enable them to engage in meaningful self-assessment. When people are free, they will be able to find their own way.

This positive view of human nature has important implications for therapeutic performance. Because of the belief that the person has the natural ability to move from mental retardation to physical therapy, the therapist places great responsibility on the client. A person-centered approach rejects the role of the therapist as a more informed authority and an inactive client who simply follows what the therapist says. Treatment is therefore based on the client's awareness and decision-making ability.

The therapist focuses on the positive aspects of human nature, on what is good for the person, and on the material that people bring to the therapist. It focuses on how clients interact with their world and others, how they can move forward in constructive ways, and how they can best deal with the obstacles (both external and external) that hinder their growth. The implication is that treatment is more than kwez professional ‖, and this treatment is not just about solving problems. Instead, psychologists aim to challenge their clients to make changes that will lead to a fuller and more real life, recognizing that this lifestyle requires ongoing struggle. People never get to the point where they can pretend to be real; rather, the best is always getting involved in the process of making them real.

2 BASIC CHARACTERISTICS

An individual-centered approach focuses on customer responsibility and the ability to find ways to fully meet reality. Clients, who know themselves better, are the ones who will find the most appropriate behavior based on growing self-esteem.

This approach emphasizes the wonderful world of the client. In an effort to capture the internal framework of client reference, therapists are primarily concerned with the client's personal and global perspective, the principles of personalized treatment apply to those who work at general levels and those who experience a high degree of mental retardation.

In a person-centered way, psychotherapy is just one example of a constructive personal relationship. Clients experience psychotherapeutic growth during and through relationships with someone who helps them do what they can do on their own. Relationships with an equally accepting, and empathetic counselor that gives the client a therapeutic change. Person-centered theory states that the therapist's job is to be present and accessible to the client and to focus on what is happening here and now.

Personalized therapy is not a collection of techniques or theories. Focused on the collection of attitudes and beliefs that the therapist exhibits, it is perhaps best seen as a way to be present and a shared journey where both therapists and clients express their personality and participate in growth experiences.

THERAPEUTIC PROCESS

1 THERAPEUTIC GOALS

An individual-centered approach aims at a greater degree of independence and individual integration. It focuses on the individual, not on the individual's silent problem. In Roger's view, the goal of treatment is not simply to solve problems. Instead, it is to help clients in their growth process, so that they can better deal with the problems they may face and the problems of the future.

The primary purpose of treatment is to provide a climate management solution to help a person become a fully functional person. Before clients can work on that goal, they must first follow the mask they are wearing, developing it through social media. Clients realize that they are no longer communicating with themselves through the previous ones. In the case of safety in the treatment regimen, they also realize that there are other opportunities. Rogers describes people who do real things, such as (1) openness of experience (2) confidence in them (3) an internal source of testing, and (4) a determination to keep growing. Promoting these features is the basic goal of individualized therapy. The therapist does not select specific client goals. The basis of a person-centered theory is the idea that client-related clients have the power to define and clarify their goals.

2 THERAPISTS FUNCTION AND ROLE

The role of a person-centered therapist is based on their lifestyle and attitude, not on strategies designed to make the client 'do something'. Research into personalized therapy seems to show that the therapist's attitudes, rather than his or her knowledge, ideas, or strategies, make it easier to change the client's personality. Basically, therapists use themselves as a tool for change. When they meet a client on a personal level, ‖their role‖ is not to have roles. Their job is to create a therapeutic climate that helps the client grow. The personalized therapist therefore creates a supportive relationship where the client gains the necessary freedom to explore areas of his or her life that are now denied awareness or distorted. By applying therapists' attitudes of genuine care, respect, acceptance, and understanding, they are able to release defenses and strong opinions and go to a higher level of personal performance.

3 CLIENT'S EXPERIENCE IN THERAPY:

Clients come to a counselor who is in a state of incompatibility, that is, there is a difference between their perceptions and their true knowledge. One of the reasons a client seeks treatment for a feeling of basic helplessness, inability, and inability to make decisions or manage their life effectively. They may hope to find a "way" through the teachings of a physician. Within a person-centered framework, however, they soon learn that they can be accountable to the relationship and can learn to relax through relationships to gain greater self-understanding. As counseling progresses, clients are able to explore a wide range of their feelings.

Gradually, they discovered hidden features inside of them. As clients feel understood and accepted, their self-defense is unnecessary, and they are very open to their experience. Because they are less threatened, they feel safer, and less vulnerable, they become more realistic, they see others with greater accuracy, and they are better able to understand and accept others. They become more self-conscious as they are, and their behavior shows more flexibility and creativity. They diminish the tendency to meet the expectations of others, and thus begin to behave in a way that is real to them. They move in such a way that they become more connected to what they are experiencing now, less of a bondage in the past, less willingness, more freedom to make decisions, and more and more confident that they will manage their lives successfully. In short, their experience in medicine is like throwing away the chains that bind them and locks them in a mental prison. With the growth of freedom they are often mentally mature and realistic.

SIX CONDITIONS ACCOUNTING FOR PERSONALITY CHANGE

Roger emphasizes that personality and behavioral changes occur when the underlying medical conditions are present. According to him, the following six conditions are necessary and sufficient for personality changes to take place:

· Two people are mentally connected. The first, which we will call the client, meets the compliance.

· The second person, whom we will call a therapist, accompanies or integrates into his or her relationship.

· The therapist receives good quality conditional or genuine client care.

· The therapist gains a sensible understanding of the internal framework of the client reference and tries to communicate this experience with the client.

· Communicating with the therapist's client with understanding and unconditional positive care is at a minimum level achieved.

Circumstances do not vary depending on the type of client. Moreover, they are necessary and adequate for all forms of treatment and apply to all personal relationships, not just to psychotherapy. The therapist does not need special knowledge.

ROLE OF THE COUNSELLOR

In Rogers' view, client / therapeutic relationships are equally visible, because therapists do not keep their information confidential or try to hide the treatment process. The process of change in the client depends, to a large extent, on the quality of this equitable relationship. As clients hear the therapist listen in a receptive way to them, they gradually learn to listen to themselves. As they find the therapist caring for them and appreciating them (even the subtleties that are considered negative), they begin to see the value and importance in them. Recognizing the reality of the therapist, they discard much of their hypocrisy and are real to both the therapist and the therapist. (2) unconditional good judgment, and (3) accurate understanding of empathy.

The congruence means that real healers, that is, real, inclusive, and authentic within the hour of treatment. They do not have a false front, their inner experience and external knowledge of the same experience, and they can freely express the feelings and attitudes that exist in a client relationship.

The second attitude therapists need to talk to a client is deep and genuine care as a person. Care is unconditional, because it is not contaminated by examining or judging a client's feelings, thoughts, and actions as good or bad. Number the therapist and warmly welcome the client without setting conditions for admission. It is not a situation if —I will accept you if... ‖, rather, it is another —I will accept you as you are‖. Receiving recognition of the client's right to emotions; it is not the authorization of all morality. All public conduct should not be tolerated or condoned. Research shows that _when 'the greater the level of care, reward, acceptance, and appreciation of the client in a non-authoritarian manner, _the more likely' the treatment will be. Feel the deep and considerate understanding of client and client. It is a sense of identity with the client. Therapists are able to share the client's world by humbly submitting to their client's feelings. Healers, however, should not lose sight of their differences. Rogers believes that when therapists are able to capture the client's private world, as the client sees and hears them, without losing the identity difference, constructive change is possible.

APPLICATION

In a person-centered framework ‖ Strategies ‖ listening, accepting, respecting, understanding, and sharing. Being busy with strategies seems like breaking up relationships. Strategies should be a reliable indicator of treatment, they cannot be self-inflicted, because the counselor is not real.

Although the person-centered approach has been used primarily for individual and group counseling, it has become more widespread than treatment. Key areas of application include education, family health, leadership and management, organizational development, health care, cultural and ethnic diversity, international relations, and the pursuit of world peace.

EVALUATION

Human-centered therapy is based on the natural philosophy of human nature that sets the inherent goal of self-realization. Moreover, Roger's view of human nature is natural, that is, we build our perceptions of truth. We are encouraged to make it a reality in the reality we see.

Roger's theory is based on the assumption that clients can understand aspects of their lives that cause them to be unhappy. They also have the power to guide themselves and to create positive personal change. A person-centered approach emphasizes this personal relationship between the client and the therapist. This approach places a primary responsibility on the treatment of the client. Clients face the opportunity to decide for themselves and adapt to their own strengths.

One of the strengths of a person-centered approach is that it does not hold back and that doctors are free to create their own style of counseling. Some strategies are not the focus, instead, the mentor's attitudes are considered important.

Another limitation is how some doctors become "more focused clients" and lose the feeling of diversity. Ironically, counselors may become so focused on the client that they reduce their value as a person and thus lose their personal impact on the client.

Human-centered therapy is based on the natural philosophy of human nature that sets the inherent goal of self-realization. Moreover, Rogers' view of human nature is natural; that is, we build on our own ideas of truth. We are encouraged to make it a reality in the reality we see. Medical counseling is based on the individual, the relationship to safety and acceptance where clients stop defending themselves and accepting and incorporating traits they deny or distort. A person-centered approach emphasizes this personal relationship between the client and the therapist; therapist attitudes are more critical than knowledge, theory, or strategy. Clients are encouraged to use these relationships to express their growth potential and to become the person they choose to be.

Rogers had it, and his theory continues to play an important role in the field of counseling and psychotherapy. Rogers was instrumental in transforming medical care from strategic emphasis and reliance on the authority of therapists to that of therapeutic relationships. Among the major contributions of personalized medicine are the effects of empathy and counseling. More than any other, personal-centered therapy has shown that empathy therapists play a vital role in making constructive change for the client.

A potential limitation of this approach is that some interns and staff with a personal focus may tend to be more supportive of clients without being challenged. One limitation is that, more than any other quality the integrity of the therapist determines the strength of the therapeutic relationship. If therapists immerse their unique identity and style in a non-judgmental and indirect way, they may not harm many clients, but they may not significantly affect clients.

VI
GESTALT THEORY

Gestalt therapy is an existing, phenomenological approach, based on a system built on the premise that people should be understood in the context of their ongoing relationships with the environment. The first goal is for clients to be aware of what they are experiencing and how they are doing it. With this awareness, change is automatic. This approach is acceptable because it focuses on the client's perceptions of reality and existence because it is based on the idea that people should always be in the process of being, re-creating, and rediscovering themselves. As an existing method, Gestalt therapy gives special attention to the presence as people experience it and ensures a person's ability to grow and heal through human contact and understanding.

The basic premise of Gestalt therapy is that individuals can better cope with their health problems, especially if they take full advantage of the awareness that is taking place between them and their surroundings. Because of certain developmental problems, people come from a variety of ways to avoid problems and as a result, they reach barriers to their own growth. Treatment provides the necessary interventions and the challenge to help them move forward with integration and the more realistic presence and presence of the virus.

1 PRINCIPLES OF GESTALT THERAPY – THEORY

Gestalt therapy, developed by Perls is an existing approach based on the premise that people should find their way of life and accept personal responsibility if they hope to achieve maturity. The basic goal, first of all, is for clients to be aware of what they are experiencing and what they are doing. Clients learn that they are responsible for what they think, hear and do. A phenomenological approach to its focus on true client perceptions. The method used is because it is based here and now. As it is in the present, it involves a change between the past and the future of man. Customers are requested to bring any concerns about what was or will be, and to address these concerns directly. Therefore, this approach has to be experienced rather than intangible. In therapy, growth occurs through real communication between the therapist and the client, not through the therapist's interpretation or strategies.

Tests are performed by the therapist to increase client self-awareness. The focus is on the system rather than the content. Emphasizing what is currently happening, rather than content that is being presented by the client. Perls believed that the way people behave in the modern world was more important to themselves than why they behave the way they do.

2 THE NOW

One of the main contributions of the Gestalt method is its emphasis on learning to appreciate and fully hear the present moment (now). To help the client connect with the current situation, the Gestalt therapist asks —what‖ and —how ‖ questions rather than ‖why‖ questions. According to Perls —why ‖ questions lead to thinking and self-deception and far from the quickness of dealing with it. It leads to endless analysis about the past that only works to encourage resistance to current information.

Most people can stay for a while. When a patient begins to talk about his or her feelings such as sadness, pain or confusion, the therapist makes every effort to get the patient to experience those feelings now. However, the past is important when it is related in some way to topics that are important to one's current function. The therapist guides clients to "bring the myth here" and strive to release the feelings they have had before. For example, instead of talking to their father about past childhood trauma, clients become injured children and talk to their father directly. Through this process there is relief from injury and the power to change in understanding and resolution.

3 UNFINISHED BUSINESS

Another important concept is unfinished business or feelings that are not expressed such as anger, resentment, hatred, pain, anxiety, guilt, rejection and so on. Though emotions are not expressed, they are associated with different memories and thoughts. Because emotions are not fully recognized, they stay behind and are driven into the present life in ways that disrupt effective communication with you and others. An unfinished business persists until one experiences and experiences unspoken emotions. Neglected emotions create unnecessary emotional turmoil that encompasses current awareness.

4 PERSONALITY AS PEELING AN ONION - LAYERS OF NEUROSIS

According to Perls, in order for people to achieve mental maturity, they need to break down the five layers of neurosis. These are (1) counterfeit (2) phobic (3) impasse (4) implosive and (5) explosive. The counterfeit layer contains the reaction of others in unusual and untrue ways. This is the level at which we play games and lose roles. By acting as if we were not real people, we are trying to live up to the dream that we or others have created. The more we realize the wisdom of playing the game and the more honest we are, the more we experience frustration and pain.

In the next layer, the phobic layer, we try to avoid the emotional pain associated with seeing our traits that we would like to deny. At this point opposition emerges. We have a horrible fear that if we realize who we really are and reveal our side to others, they will surely reject us.

Below this layer is something wrong, or a point at which we are stuck in our maturity. This is a point where we assure ourselves that we have no resources within us to go beyond the concrete point without environmental support. In an argument we often feel dead and feel worthless. If we hope to feel alive, it is important that we go through this ordeal.

If we allow ourselves to fully experience our death, rather than deny it or flee from it, then the level of entry emerges. By contacting this layer, or our death and false ways, we expose our defenses and begin to connect with our true identity.

Perls asserts that retreating the explosive layer creates an explosive atmosphere. When we touch the explosive layer, we release the fake and hypocritical roles and release the vast amount of power we have been holding on to by pretending to be who we are and then living and being real.

5. CONTACT AND RESISTANCES TO CONTACT

In Gestalt therapy communication is needed in the event of change and growth. Contact is made by seeing, hearing, smelling, touching and moving. Active communication means communicating with nature and other people without losing the feeling of the individual. The requirements for good communication are clear awareness, absolute power and the ability to express oneself, rather than the final state of access to communication, can be thought of as different levels. After a communication experience there is often a withdrawal to cover what has been learned.

The Gestalt Therapist also focuses on opposing communication. In Gestalt's view resistance refers to the protections we develop to prevent us from experiencing the present in a more complete and realistic way. The five stages of neurosis represent a person's style of retaining energy open to a hypothetical service. There are also protective measures that prevent people from becoming real.

Introjection, projection, retroflection, deflection and confluence are five major channels of resistance that are challenged in Gestalt therapy.

Introjection is a tendency to be cynical about accepting the beliefs and standards of others without comparing them with what we are.

Projection is a distortion of the introductions. In this we deny certain aspects of ourselves by giving ourselves the environment.

retroflection involves giving back to us what we would like to do for another person or doing for us what we would like someone else to do for us. When we scream and hurt ourselves, for example, we tend to direct our anger inwardly so that we are afraid to direct our inner anger that we are afraid to direct toward others.

deflection is a disruptive process that makes it difficult to maintain a continuous sense of communication. Rebels try to spread their message through excessive humor, casual talk, and questions rather than statements.

Integration involves the blurring of awareness of differences between the individual and the environment. Conflict in a relationship involves the absence of conflict, or the belief that all parties have the same feelings and thoughts.

Gestalt therapist anxiety is a disorder of the environment where one does not know the process. Terms such as refusing to touch the frontier mean the elements that people are using to control their environment. The basis of

Gestalt treatment is that contact is normal and healthy.

6 ENERGY AND BLOCKS TO ENERGY

Gestalt therapy focuses on the source of energy, how it is used, and how it can be prevented. Blocked power is another form of resistance. Commenting on the value of focusing on a client's strengths in medical practice, Zinker writes that clients may not know the strengths or whereabouts, and may experience them in a negative way. In his view the best available treatment involves a strong relationship that awakens and nurtures the client without undermining the therapist's own strength.

Zinker emphasizes that it is the therapist's job to help clients find ways to block energy and help them turn this blocked energy into a flexible behavior. This process is best done when resistance can be seen as a client's refusal to cooperate and as something that should be readily available. Clients can be encouraged to see how their resistance is expressed in their bodies and instead of trying to eliminate certain physical symptoms, they can actually fully absorb the statistics of allergies. By allowing them to exaggerate in their strong mouth and by moving their legs, they can discover for themselves how they divert energy and keep themselves powerless.

THERAPEUTIC PROCESS

Gestalt therapy is an interaction between people, in which clients often travel a certain way:

- move on to more self-awareness about them
- gradually take ownership of their experience
- develop skills and acquire values that will enable them to meet their needs without infringing on the rights of others
- know all their senses
- learn to accept responsibility for their actions, including accepting the consequences of their actions
- from external support to increasing internal support
- Still be able to ask for and get help from others and give to others.

The main purpose of the Gestalt process is to raise awareness — which, in itself, seems to be therapeutic. With awareness they have the power to deal with accepting the contradictory parts of their personality and to communicate accurate information and facts.

The therapist focuses on the client's emotions, instantaneous awareness, body messages, strength, avoidance and awareness barriers. Perls has shown the opposite of wisdom, asserting that most of our thinking is a way to avoid emotions. According to Perls neurosis they do not see the obvious. They don't know if their fist is too strong, their voice is controlled, or not responding to a therapist's suggestion. The therapist's job is to challenge clients to learn to use their senses more fully and to communicate with physical messages.

An important function of the Gestalt therapist is to pay attention to the body language of the client. The therapist needs to be aware of the differences in attention and awareness as well as the conflict between words and what clients do with their bodies. In addition, the Gestalt adviser emphasizes the relationship between language patterns and personality. This form of communication suggests that the client's speech patterns are usually expressions of his or her feelings, thoughts, and emotions. Other issues that may be the basis of treatment include client-physician relationships and similarities in how clients relate to therapists and others in their area.

Miriam Polster describes a three-pronged combination sequence that demonstrates client growth in treatment. The first part of this sequence contains the discovery. Clients may gain new insights about themselves or gain a new perspective on the old situation, or they may reconsider someone who is important in their lives. The second category is accommodation, which includes clients' perception of choice. Clients first try new behaviors in a supportive environment and then increase their awareness. The third stage is analogy, which involves learning customers how to influence their site. At this stage, clients feel able to cope with the surprises they experience in everyday life. Behavior at this stage may include the client's position on a sensitive matter. Ultimately, clients develop confidence in their ability to develop and improve.

Doing Gestalt involves a person-to-person relationship between the therapist and the client. The therapist's experience, awareness and ideas provide the basis for the therapeutic process and the client's awareness and reaction are paramount.

The therapist provides feedback, especially on what clients do with their body. Feedback allows clients to develop awareness of what they are actually doing. Therapists are responsible for the quality of their presence, self-awareness and the client, and staying open to the client. They are also responsible for establishing and maintaining a therapeutic environment that will promote a spirit of professionalism on the part of the client.

APPLICATION/TECHNIQUES

Techniques can be useful tools to help the client gain fuller awareness, experience internal conflicts resolve inconsistencies and dichotomies and work through an impasse that is preventing completion of unfinished business.

1 Internal Dialogue Exercise

Gestalt therapists pay close attention to the diversity of human activity. Treatment focuses on the battle between the 'upper dog' and the 'lower dog'. The first is righteous, dictatorial, moral, demanding, authoritative, and deceptive. The latter plays the role of victim by self-defense, apology, helplessness and weakness and by making oneself vulnerable. The conflict between the two opposing poles in humanity is based on a method of presentation, which involves integrating the characteristics of others, usually parents, into one's self-centered system. It is important that if you know a person's inputs, especially those that are toxic they poison the system and prevent personal integration.

The empty seat method is a way for the client to issue an external introduction. Two chairs are used in this process when the therapist asks the client to sit in one chair and become a fully grown dog and then switch to another chair into an underdog. In fact, this is a way to play a role where all the parts are played by the client. Conflict can be resolved through client acceptance and mutual merger. This process helps clients connect with a feeling or side that they may be denying and helps them see annoying parental introductions.

2 Making rounds

This is a task that involves asking someone in the group to go up to the others in the group and talk or do something with each person. The aim is coping, risk, self-disclosure, experimentation with new behaviors and growth and change.

"I have made a commitment..."

A practical approach to extension of awareness is also designed to help customers recognize and accept their feelings instead of expressing their feelings to others. In this case, the therapist may ask the client to make a statement and add eseand commit myself ‖. Eg, — I feel lonely and committed to my loneliness‖.

It plays a guess

A therapist asks a person who says "I don't trust you" to play the role of an untrustworthy person - that is, someone else - in order to determine the level at which infidelity is internal conflict.

3 Retreat strategy

The therapist may ask someone who claims to be suffering from severe obstacles and extreme anxiety to play a role in the show. This process helps clients begin to accept certain personalities and try to deny them.

4 Exercise activity

Internal practice consumes a lot of energy and often impairs our self-esteem and our willingness to try new behaviors. Members of the medical team can share their trials to learn more about the many preparation methods they use to strengthen their community roles.

5 Excessive work

The person is asked to exaggerate by repeatedly touching or touching or verbally abusing the word, which often reinforces the moral impression and makes the inner meaning clear.

For example, if a patient reports that his or her legs are shaking, the therapist may ask the client to stand up and exaggerate the tremor.

6 Sitting and feeling

When a client refers to an unpleasant feeling or attitude and a strong desire to escape, the therapist urges the client to stay with him or her to keep that feeling.

7 Gestalt method of dream work

The Gestalt method does not define and interpret a dream. Rather, the purpose is to rekindle the dream and bring it back to life as if it were happening now. Because each part of the dream is thought to be your own manifestation, the person creates the clues between the letters or the various parts. By engaging in conversation between these conflicting parties, one gradually becomes more aware of the scope of one's emotions.

Gestalt therapy is an experience therapy that emphasizes awareness here and now. The main focus is on that and the ethics and role of the unfinished business from the past that hinders successful operations in the present. Some of the most important principles of how to do it are to accept personal responsibility, living at that time and a positive attitude against vague talk about information. This approach helps clients deal with avoidance, unfinished business and issues. Increasing awareness is a basic goal. With awareness, clients are able to adapt polarity and reconnect all their features.

It is a practice with a range of trials and exercises. This approach is a vision for growth and development, not just a strategic plan to treat disorders. It also has great creative power. Gestalt experiments can be tailored to fit the unique way a person perceives and interprets his or her culture.

The main criticism of the Perlsian style of Gestalt treatment involves its emphasis on the psychological aspects of personality. In addition for Gestalt tests to be effective, clients must be prepared. Gestalt techniques tend to produce a high level of deep emotion. This focus on touch, there are certain clear boundaries for those clients who are placed in a state of emotional restraint. Strategies designed to increase client awareness and help it experiment with new behaviors. These methods are the only way to help people change, not just themselves. Many strategies are contradictory. Counselors need to be proactive and challenging and clients must be willing to take risks and challenge themselves.

Gestalt Therapy is an experience that emphasizes current awareness and quality of communication between individuals and the environment. The main focus is to help the client realize how behaviors that have been a part of strategic rehabilitation in the past may affect the effectiveness and efficiency of the present. The goal of the approach, first and foremost, is to raise awareness. Another purpose of treatment is to assist clients in assessing how they interact with their local environment. Changes occur with the highest awareness of — what.‖ The therapist works with the client to identify statistics, or the most important individual characteristics - the field of practice, as they appear in the background. The Gestalt therapist believes that each client is able to control themselves if those statistics are co-ordinated and resolved so that others can change them. The role of Gestalt therapist is to help clients identify the most pressing issues, needs, and interests and to design tests that sharpen those figures or that test resistance and communication awareness.

Another contribution to Gestalt treatment is the exciting way in which the past is handled in a fun way by bringing the right aspects to the present.

Therapists challenge clients with creative ways to identify and work with problems that impede current performance. In addition, paying attention to the obvious verbal and non-verbal cues provided to clients is a useful way to tackle a counseling session. Focused on growth and development rather than a strategic plan to treat disorders. Gestalt therapy is the perfect way to value each aspect of your individual experience equally. Therapists allow the mathematical process to guide them. They do not reach customers with a predetermined set of bias or an agenda set. Rather, they are emphasizing what happens on the boundary between man and nature. A key strength of Gestalt therapy is the effort to integrate theory, practice, and research.

Most of my criticism of Gestalt treatment is about the old version, or Fritz Perls' style, which emphasizes addressing and highlighting the psychological aspects of personality. For Gestalt treatment to be effective, the therapist must have a high level of personal development. Recognizing personal needs and seeing that they do not interfere with the client's process, current presence, and willingness to not protect and expose themselves all require a lot of therapy. There is a risk that untrained therapists will become particularly concerned about impressive clients.

VII
REALITY THEORY

Physicians believe that the underlying problem of many clients is the same - they are involved in an unsatisfactory relationship that exists or they lack what might be called a relationship. Many client problems are caused by not being able to connect, be close to others, or having satisfying or successful relationships with at least one important person in their lives. The therapist directs clients to a satisfying relationship and teaches them to behave in a more effective way than they do now. The more clients you can communicate with, the more likely they are to be happy. True treatment is based on a choice of choice. Choice theory explains why and how it works, and true treatment offers a delivery system to help people manage their lives more effectively. Treatment consists primarily of teaching clients to make effective decisions as they interact with the people they need in their lives.

REALITY THEORY

William Glasser who was psycho analytically trained, quickly became disenchanted with this approach, and began to experiment with innovative methods, which later came to be called reality therapy. Glasser's early work focused on asking clients to recognize and take responsibility for what they were doing in the present, rather than dwelling on what they had done, thought, or felt in the past.

In reality therapy clients are asked to identify their wants and needs. Additionally, they are challenged to evaluate their behaviour, formulate a plan for change, commit themselves to such a plan, and follow through with their commitment. By avoiding making excuses and blaming others and by evaluating what they are doing to get what they want, they are able to achieve increasing control over their life.

A basic assumption of Glasser's approach is that everyone has a —*growth force*‖; this force impels one to develop a —success identity‖ (viewing oneselfas being worthy of love and as being a significant person). A further assumption is that any change in one‘s identity is contingent on behavioural change. Like behaviour therapy, transactional analysis, and rational emotive therapy, reality therapy is an active, directive, and didactic model. It stresses present behaviour, not attitudes, insight, one‘s past, or unconscious motivations.

1 Human needs and purposeful behaviour

William Glasser identifies four essential psychological needs *belonging, power, freedom, and fun* and the physiological need for survival.**Control theory** explains how we attempt to satisfy these basis needs, which are thepowerful forces that drive us.

People develop an inner —*picture album"* of specific wants that contains precise snapshots of how they wish to fulfill their needs. A major goal of reality therapy is to teach people better ways of fulfilling their needs and to help them effectively get what they want from life.

Responsibility consists of learning how to realistically meet these basic psychological needs, and the essence of therapy consists of teaching people to accept that responsibility. People behave for a purpose: to mold their environment as sculptor molds clay, matching their own inner pictures of what they want. These goals are achievable only through hard work

2 Existential/Phenomenological Orientation

In many ways Glasser's approach is based on phenomenological and existing structures. He emphasizes that we see the world as we really are, not as we really are. It is important for clinicians to understand that clients live in a foreign country and in their own inner world.

Glasser does not accept the idea that grief just happens to us instead, it is a matter of choice. He notes that consumers are often quick to complain that they are upset because the people in their lives are not behaving the way they want in the world. It is important to reorganize that all behaviors are selected, which includes feeling sad and thinking they are victims. People choose grief in an effort to alleviate their frustration.

- Managing anger
- Making others help
- Forgive their reluctance to do something effective, as well
- For strong control

Glasser talks about people who are depressed or irritable, rather than depressed or angry. From this perspective, stress can be defined as the active choice they make rather than the result of being an inactive victim. This oku repression qubo process ensures anger, and allows them to call for help. Glasser insists that as long as people hold to the idea that they are victims of depression and that grief is something that happens to them, they will not change for the better. They can only change

when they see and act according to the fact that what they are doing is the result of their choice.

3 Code of Conduct

According to Glasser's formulation of control theory (1985), humans are constantly in control of what they do. This basic premise is enshrined in the context of understanding its holistic behavior, which always consists of four parts; acting (or active behavior such as speaking or running); thinking (voluntary thoughts and statements); feelings such as anger, joy, depression, anxiety); and physiology (such as sweating, ‖a headache‖, or developing other psychological symptoms).

Wubbolding uses the —ipotimende‖ metaphor to describe the concept of complete morality. When you lift the suitcase hold it by the easy part, the handle. Perfect behavior is like a suitcase. The handle is part of the make-up. Raise the handle and the whole behavior following the sequence of actions, thinking, emotion and physiology. It is often easier to force ourselves to do something different than to hear or think something different.

Control theory is based on the assumption that it is impossible to choose the perfect behavior and not choose all your components. If whole behavior is expected to change (such as dealing with the emotional and physical effects of stress), then it is necessary to change what a person is doing and thinking. For example, a person may feel frustrated and depressed if he cannot get the job he has applied for. A person does not have the ability to directly change how he feels, other than what he does and the ability to change what he thinks no matter how he may feel. Therefore, to continue to change perfect behavior lies in choosing to change what they do. When a person makes a significant change in part of the process he will not be able to avoid changing his thoughts, feelings, and genetic makeup.

4 Success Ownership and Good Addiction

The primary goal of virtual therapy is to help people find effective ownership. Those who have a successful personality find themselves able to give and receive love, to feel valued by others, to feel valued, to deal with others in a caring way, and to satisfy their own needs in life. ways that are not at the expense of others.

Those seeking treatment tend to be people who ―main ownership of failure‖. They feel unloved, rejected, and unwanted, unable to get along with others, unable to act and cling to commitments, and often helpless.

Often people with unsuccessful ownership face challenges in despair ―I can not‖‖, a self-fulfilling prophecy that leads to further lack of success, which also supports a negative self-image and ultimately makes these people see themselves as hopeless failures. in life. Because reality therapy assumes that humans ultimately are self-determined beings who become what they decide to be, the program is designed to teach people how to change behaviors that promote failed self-esteem and develop behaviors that lead to successful ownership.

5 Summary of Management Theory

Control theory is based on the premise that morality is the control of our ideas. Although a person may not be able to control what is in the real world, he tries to control his thoughts to meet his needs. In this process man creates his inner world.

Everything people do, think, and hear is based on what happens inside them. In other words, a person's feelings are not controlled by others or events. People are not psychological slaves to others, unless they choose to be. No matter what the circumstances, what one does, what one thinks, and what one feels is always their best effort at the moment to satisfy the inner strength. People can easily choose better behavior if they find that what they are doing, thinking and feeling does not just happen to them but that they are really making decisions`

6 Definition of ethical selection theory

Selective theory means that everything we do from birth to death is moral and, without exception, everything we do is selective. All perfect behavior is our best effort to find what we need to satisfy our needs. Integrity teaches that all behaviors are made up of four separate and distinct parts — actions, thoughts, feelings, and physical structures — that interact with all our actions, thoughts, and emotions. Morality is meaningful because it is designed to bridge the gap between what we want and what we see. Positive behavior is always produced in this variation. Our behavior comes from within, and thus we choose our destiny.

Glasser states that talking about depression, headaches, irritability, or anxiety means doing nothing and not taking personal responsibility, and it is inaccurate. It is more appropriate to think of these as part of a holistic behavior and to use relaxing actions, headaches, anger, and anxiety to express oneself. It is far better to think of people who are depressed or irritable than to be depressed or angry. When people choose grief by developing "painful" behaviors, it is because these good behaviors cannot be instantly established, and these behaviors often get what they want.

When a reality therapist starts teaching choice theory, the client often complains and says, —I'm suffering, don't tell me I choose to suffer like this.‖ Although it hurts to be depressed, the therapist explains that people are suffering. do not choose pain and suffering directly; rather, it is a non-selective part of their total behavior. Human behavior is the best, most ineffective, effort to meet needs.

Robert Wubbolding added a new perspective to selection theory. He believes that morality is language, and that we send messages about what we do. The purpose of morality is to persuade the world to get what we want. Therapists ask clients what messages they send to the world through their actions: —What message do you want others to receive? ‖ —What message do others receive that you intended to send or not? ‖ Considering the messages clients receive? referrals, counselors can help clients indirectly gain greater appreciation for the messages they send to others unintentionally.

7 Features of Real Treatment

Contemporary reality therapy quickly focuses on unsatisfactory relationships or lack of relationships, which is often the cause of customer problems. Consumers may complain about a problem such as poor job performance, poor performance at school, or a lack of meaningful relationships. When clients complain that other people are hurting them, the therapist is not involved in finding fault. Real therapists ask clients to consider how effective their choices are, especially as these options affect their relationships with people who are important in their lives. Selection theory teaches that it makes no sense to talk about what clients cannot control; which emphasizes what clients can control in the relationship. The basic axiom for choosing a theory, which is important for customers to understand, is: —The only person you can control is yourself.‖

True healers do not listen for very long to complaints, suspicions, and criticisms, because these are the most ineffective behaviors in our moral chain. Because real therapists pay little attention to these harmful behaviors, they often disappear from treatment. What do real healers focus on? Here are some basic features of true healing.

Selection theory changes the focus of the obligation on selection and selection. Real therapists treat people — as if ‖ have a choice. Therapists focus on those areas where clients have a choice, because doing so brings them closer to people in need. For example, engaging in meaningful activities, such as work, is a great way to earn the respect of other people, and work can help clients fulfill their energy need. It is very difficult for adults to feel happy about themselves if they do not participate in some kind of meaningful work. As clients begin to feel happier about it, it is less necessary for them to continue to choose unhealthy and self-destructive behavior.

True healers strive to be the best in their profession. For themselves, therapists can use relationships to teach clients how to connect with others in their lives. Glasser argues that money transfer is a way for both therapists and clients to avoid becoming who they are and to own what they are currently doing. It does not make sense for therapists to come up with the idea of who they are but themselves. Suppose a client says, —I see you as a father or a mother and that is why I behave the way I do.‖ In such a situation a true therapist can say clearly and firmly, —I am not your mother, father, or anyone but me.

Some clients come to counseling convinced that their problems started in the past and should revisit the past if they are to be helped. Glasser asserts that we are the product of our past but insists that we are not victims of the past unless we choose to be one. Nevertheless, many therapeutic models continue to teach that in order to be effective in the present we must understand and revisit the past. Glasser disagrees with this belief and asserts that any mistakes made in the past do not apply now. We can only satisfy our needs right now.

The reality therapist does not completely reject the past. If the client wants to talk about past successes or good relationships in the past, the therapist will listen because this may be repeated in the present. Real therapists will devote just enough time to previous failures to reassure clients that they are not rejecting it. As soon as possible, therapists tell clients: —What happened is over; it cannot be changed. The more we look back, the more we avoid looking ahead. " Although the past has pushed us to the present, it does not have to determine our future.

Glasser argues that people with symptoms believe that if they did not have symptoms they would be happier. Whether people are distressed or depressed, they often feel that their experiences are normal. They are reluctant to accept the fact that their suffering is a result of their perfect conduct. Their symptoms can be viewed as a physical warning that their behavior does not meet their basic needs. Reality Therapist spends as little time as possible with symptoms because they will last longer if needed to deal with an unsatisfactory relationship or frustration with basic needs.

Selective theory dispels the traditional notion that people with symptoms of physical and mental illness are mentally ill. Glasser (2003) warned people to beware of mental illnesses, which can be harmful to a person's physical and mental health. He criticizes the development of traditional psychiatry by relying heavily on DSM-IV-TR in both diagnosis and treatment. Glasser (2003) challenges traditional beliefs about mental illness and treatment through medication. He asserts that psychotherapy often has negative effects on physical and mental health.

THERAPEUTIC PROCESS

Eight Stage Model:

Glasser originally conceptualized reality therapy in eight steps:

- Make friends or get involved, or get alone: create relationship or give rapport
- De-emphasize the client's history and find out what you are doing now.
- Help the client learn to make an evolution of his or her behaviour. Help the client find out if what he or she is saying is really helpful.
- Once you have evaluated the behaviour, then you can begin to explore alternative behaviours. Behaviours that may prove more helpful.
- Get a commitment to a plan of change.
- Maintain an attitude of —no excuses if you don't do it‖.by now the client is committed to the change and must learn to be responsible in carrying it out.
- Be tough without punishment. Teach people to do things without being punished if they do not; it creates a more positive motivation.
- Refuse to give up Once clients realize the counsellor will not give up, they feel more support and work proceeds with more efficiency and promise.

THERAPEUTIC PROCEDURES

The practice of physical therapy begins with the counselor's efforts to create a supportive environment in which clients can begin to make changes in their lives. Counselors always try to focus on what they are doing now.

They also refrain from discussing clients' feelings or physiology as if these were separate from their complete behavior. They help their clients see the connection between what they hear and their actions and thoughts. Real therapists do not accept excuses for indifference and show clients that excuses arise from self-deception that may provide temporary relief but ultimately lead to failure and perceived failure.

Part of a therapist's job is to explore a client's 'photo album' and how their behavior is aimed at bringing their vision of the outside world closer to their inner world of what they want. Physical therapy emphasizes current behavior and focuses on transforming current whole behaviors, not just mental and emotional states. Past events are only worrying as they influence how the client behaves now. Clients are helped to identify specific ways to meet their needs. The process of creating and making plans is how people gain control of their lives. The purpose of the strategy is to plan a successful experience. Throughout this planning phase the consultant continues to urge clients to take responsibility for their choices and actions.

1 Procedures that lead to change

The practice of physical therapy can best be thought of as a cycle of counseling, consisting of two main components: (1) creating a place of counseling and (2) applying certain processes that lead to a change in behavior. The art of counseling is to integrate these components in ways that lead clients to evaluate their own lives and decide to go the most effective way.

The psychological counseling cycle begins with building working relationships with clients. The process continues by examining the needs, requirements, and opinions of customers. Clients assess their overall behavior and evaluate how successful they are in getting what they want. When clients decide to try new behaviors, they make plans that will lead to change, and commit to those strategies. The psychological counseling cycle includes tracking how well clients are performing and providing additional consultation as needed.

The art of practicing physical therapy involves much more than just following the procedures in the form of a step-by-step recipe book. Although these processes are described in simple, non-jargon, they can be challenging to implement.

The practice of physical therapy is based on the assumption that a supportive and challenging environment allows clients to begin to make lifestyle changes. Therapeutic relationships are the basis of active practice; if this is lacking, there is little hope that the system can be used successfully.

According to Glasser (1992), the processes leading to change are based on the assumption that people are motivated to change (1) when they are convinced that their current behavior is not getting what they want and (2) where they believe. they can choose other behaviors that will bring them closer to what they want.

2 Program "WDEP"

The term WDEP is used to describe processes that are critical to the effectiveness of physical therapy. The WDEP physical therapy program can be used to help clients evaluate their needs, potential limitations, self-assessment opportunities, and development planning programs (Wubbolding, 2007a, 2007b). Each character refers to a set of strategies: W = needs and requirements; D = direction and performance; E = self-examination; and P = editing. These strategies are designed to encourage change.

Wanted (Testing requirements, requirements, and ideas)

Real therapists help clients find their needs and hopes. All requirements are related to five basic requirements. They ask, —What do you want? ‖ By asking the therapist about the skill, clients are helped to define what they want in the counseling system and the world around them. It is helpful for clients to explain what they expect and want from the counselor as well as for themselves. Part of the consultation process involves exploring —the photo album, ‖ or the world of quality, customer and how their behavior is intended to bring their vision of the outside world closer to their inner world of what they want.

Clients are given the opportunity to explore every aspect of their lives, including what they want from their family, friends, and work. In addition, this assessment of needs, requirements, and ideas should continue throughout the counseling process as customer images change.

Guidance and Performance

True therapy emphasizes current behavior and only relates to past events as they influence how clients behave now. Focusing on the present is reflected in the question often asked by a reality therapist: —What are you doing? ‖ Although problems may be caused in the past, clients need to learn how to deal with them in the present by learning better. ways to get what they want. The past can be debated if doing so will help clients plan for a better future. The challenge for the therapist is to help clients make the most satisfying choices.

At the beginning of counseling it is important to consult with clients throughout their lives, including where they are going and where their behavior is taking them. This test is the precursor to the next test to see if it is the preferred method. The therapist holds a mirror in front of a client and asks, —What do you see now and in the future? True healing focuses on raising awareness and transforming current behaviors.

The essence of reality therapy is to ask clients to evaluate the following: —Is your current behavior more likely to get what you want now, and will take you where you want to go? . According to Wubbolding, clients often bring problems with important relationships, which are the source of their dissatisfaction. A counselor can help clients evaluate their behavior by asking this question: —Does your current behavior bring you closer to people or more important to you? ‖

True therapists may be a guide for certain clients at the start of treatment. This is to help clients see that certain behaviors are not working. In dealing with troubled clients, for example, it is sometimes necessary to specify exactly what will work and what will not. Some clients, such as alcoholics and children of alcohol addicts, need guidance at the beginning of the treatment period, because they often do not have the means to think in their control system to be able to make consistent assessments that their lives are out of control. . These clients may have blurry images, and, at times, I do not know what they are looking for or whether the things they want are real. As they grow older and continue to interact with the mentor, they learn to do experiments with minimal help from the mentor.

The WDEP program can be used to help people meet their basic needs and in the context of the group. Reality therapy applies to individual counseling, marriage and family therapy, group counseling, social work, education, disaster intervention, rehabilitation and rehabilitation, institutional management and community development. Most military clinics that treat drug and alcohol abusers use physical therapy as the treatment of their choice. This treatment is effective for people with any type of mental illness. It is used by children, teenagers, adults and the elderly. According to Glaser, the only factor that limits its effectiveness is the therapeutic skill of the therapist.

Planning and Action

Much of the important work of the counseling process in this process involves helping clients identify specific ways to meet their needs and requirements. When clients decide what they want to change, they are usually ready to explore other behaviors and make an application. The process of creating and programming enables people to begin to manage their lives more effectively. If the system does not work, for whatever reason, the consultant and the client work together to create a different system. The program gives the client a priority, but plans can be changed as needed.

Wubbolding discusses the key role of planning and commitment. The end of the counseling cycle depends on the action plan. He uses

SAMIC3 summary to capture the essence of a good program: simple, accessible, measurable, fast, editor-controlled, committed, and continuous.

A reality therapist works as a teacher, mentor, and model, dealing with clients in ways that help them assess what they are doing and whether their behavior meets their basic needs without harming themselves or others. The heart of true medicine learns to make better and more effective decisions and to gain effective control. People are in control of their lives rather than being victims of circumstances beyond their control. Practical medical professionals focus on what clients know and are willing to do right now to change their behavior. Staff teach clients how to make important connections with others. Therapists continue to ask clients to evaluate the effectiveness of their options to determine if the best option is possible.

The practice of physical therapy involves two parts, the area of counseling and certain processes that lead to a change in behavior. This treatment process empowers clients to go the extra mile to get what they want. The goals of physical therapy include behavioral change, better decision-making, improved relationships, improved quality of life, and effective satisfaction of all psychological needs.

Among the benefits of physical therapy are its short-term focus and the fact that it deals with careful behavioral problems. The existing foundations of selective theory are the great strength of this approach. People who are considered depressed and hopeless. Instead, people are considered to be doing their best, or making decisions that they hope will result in the fulfillment of their needs.

One of the main drawbacks of physical therapy is that it does not adequately emphasize the role of these aspects of the counseling process: the role of understanding, ignorance, and power of the past and the impact of traumatic experiences on childhood. , the importance of dream therapy, and the place of transmission. Because physical therapy is almost entirely based on knowledge, it does not take into account factors such as conflict and the power of unconsciousness to influence how we think, feel, behave, and choose.

VIII

BEHAVIOURAL COUNSELLING: PHILOSOPHY AND EXERCISE

Behavioral counseling views your performance as centered on assessment-based learning principles. This model provides a greater degree of clarity in visual analysis, as compared to intrapsychic, human behavior than that offered by human, existing, or psychological models.

The term behavioral therapy refers to the use of a variety of strategies and procedures based on different learning theories. The basic concept of moral perception is that all problematic behaviors, perceptions and emotions are learned and that they can be replaced with new learning. It also thinks that behavior exposing clients is a problem. Successful resolution of these problematic behaviors solves the problem. This approach is different from relationship-focused and comprehensive approaches that place greater emphasis on clients 'gaining an understanding of their problems as a requirement for change. Behavior assumes that change can occur without understanding and that behavioral changes may lead to a growing level of self-awareness.

This way

· Focuses on selecting targeted behaviors that need to be changed and defined the type of desired change

• Investigates visible events in the environment that maintain morality

• It clearly identifies both local changes and interventions that can change behavior

• Emphasis on data-based assessment and treatment emergence

• Ask the question — Once new behaviors have been developed, how can they be maintained and adapted to new conditions over time?

Three areas of development

Modern behavioral therapy can be understood by considering three major areas of development of classical conditioning, functional status and psychotherapy. First is the classical conditioning method in which certain respondents' treatment, such as kneeling and saliva, is released from an inactive substance. This approach was based on HULLIAN learning of the theory and nature of PAVLOVIAN (or classical). Second is the operational conditioning method. Employee behavior includes actions that work locally to produce results. Examples of practical behavior include reading, writing, driving and eating utensils. Such behavior involves most of the important responses we make in everyday life. When the natural changes brought about in a behavior intensify (if they give a certain reward to the body and remove the opposing motives) the changes confirm that the behavior will recur. If environmental changes are not productive, changes are slowed down so that behavior can recur B.F.SKINNER was studying the application of the operating principle.

Fixing. Skinner's view of behavior control is based on the principles of work ethic based on the assumption that behavioral changes are brought about when those behaviors are followed by a particular type of outcome. Skinner asserts that learning will not happen without some kind of reinforcement, good or bad. To him the strengthened actions are often repeated, and the depressed ones are often extinguished. This model is based on consolidation principles and aims to identify the factors that control the environment that lead to behavioral change.

Good reinforcement is the process by which the response is followed by the presentation of motivation. It involves the addition of something (such as praise or money) as a result of a particular behavior. Encouragement is a good boost, which the body needs, such a diet. Negative reinforcement involves the removal of unpleasant motives in a situation where certain behaviors have occurred. Negative assurances are often unpleasant, so that a person is motivated to do what he wants to do to avoid an unpleasant situation.

Third is the mental tendency in behavioral therapy. Your behavioral model of both classic and operanti-conditioning models does not include any reference in meditation thoughts (such as the role of thought processes, attitudes and values) perhaps as a reaction against psychodynamic approaches that focus on understanding. Since the 1970s the behavioral movement has allowed for a more conducive environment for thinking, to the point of providing cognitive features that play an important role in understanding and treating behavioral problems. Mental-behavioral therapy has now been established as part of standard behavioral therapy. Behavioral therapy has undergone significant changes and is on the increase. It is no longer focused on reading theory alone, nor is it a set of less-defined strategies. Modern behavioral therapy incorporates different perspectives, research methods, and therapeutic approaches to define and modify behavior.

PAVLOV'S CLASSICAL CONDITIONING

Classical conditioning refers to what happens before learning that creates a response by comparing. An important figure in the area was Ivan Pavlov who demonstrated the ancient nature of experiments with dogs. Putting food in the dog's mouth leads to saliva, which is the behavior of the respondents. When food is introduced repeatedly with some initial neutral motive (something that does not produce a specific response), such as a bell ring, the dog will eventually collapse due to the ringing of the bell alone. However, if the bell rings repeatedly but can not be combined with food, the saliva response will work

eventually they shrink and disappear. An example of a process based on the historical model is Joseph Wolpe's systematic densitization. This app shows how the learning principles found in a test laboratory can be used in a clinic. Allergies may be applied to people who, through a history of the past, develop a strong fear of flying after having a frightening experience while flying.

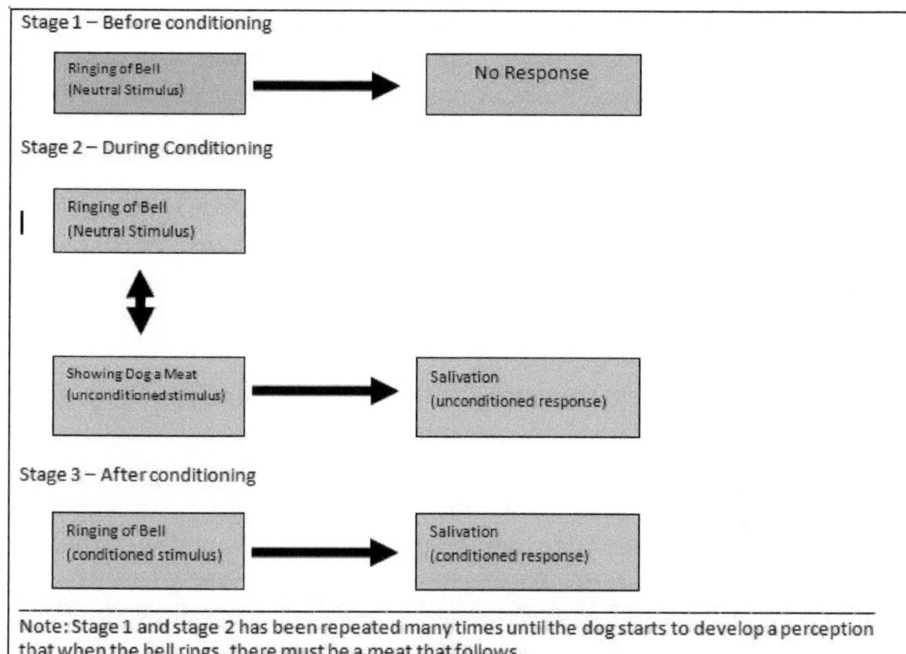

Diagrammatic representation of Pavlov's experiments

WATSON'S CONDITIONED BEHAVIOURISM

John B. Watson believed that there were two ideologies that dominated American psychology in his day: introspective or subjective psychology, which he called the old psychology and the new purpose of moral psychology. Concepts such as awareness and self-examination, the subject of old psychology, were magical. Psychology, as a targeted and explored branch of natural science, requires less such concepts as chemistry and physics. Just as animal behavior can be investigated without reference to knowledge, so too can human behavior be investigated. Watson devoted nearly 12 years to animal experimentation and noted that it was natural for him to be drawn into a theory instead of his experimental work.

The Watsonian ethnographer sees all psychological problems and their solutions as organized in terms of motivation and response, often abbreviated as S-R. Stimuli may be unconditional because from birth they call for specific responses, such as removing the eyes or closing the eyes from the light. On the other hand, many of the things that motivate people to respond are based on or read.

Watson believed that, given the full control of twelve healthy babies from birth, he could take randomly and train him to be any type of person he could choose, be it a doctor, a lawyer, an artist, a beggar or a thief. Inheritance of strength, talent, attitude, mental structure and traits do not really exist, because these things depend on training.

Watson described how emotions are corrected. According to him, there are three types of unreadable beginnings for emotional reactions, or unlearned emotional responses to motivation. These answers are fear, anger and love. These emotional reactions can be considered unconditional intelligence or responses. For example, loud noise is an important stimulant to arouse fear. Watson demonstrated this with a series of experiments on an 11-month-old baby named Albert in which he developed a boy's emotional reaction to the fear of a white mouse. He achieved this by linking to some of the temptations of the loud banging of the bar when Albert touched the white mouse. Later when the mouse was introduced on its own, Albert showed a fearful reaction to crying, falling and crawling away.

Watson argued that 'thinking' refers to all the behaviors of subordinate words. That is, thinking is like talking alone. And in some cases, such as a reaction to a new situation, a person's thinking is similar to the behavior of a mouse in a maze. When subjects are asked to think logically it is easy to see how they have solved their problem with word behavior. Memory is regarded as maintaining speech patterns. When people come across a stimulus and after a while they make a general thought they have learned to do when the stimulus starts to exist.

Watson described personality as amba the amount of work that can be achieved through actual ethical observation over a sufficient period of time to provide reliable information. In other words, personality is the ultimate product of our habits, according to Watson. Thus, personality is defined as behavior or behavior that can be precisely perceived and that can lead to accurate predictions of future behavior. He suggested five ways to get a more accurate measure of personality, namely by reading (a) individual education chart, (b) success chart, (c) leisure time and record of recreation,

(d) emotional formation under real-life situations and (e) responses to tests psychological. Personality problems are behavioral disorders and behavioral conflicts that need to be eliminated unconditionally and corrected.

SKINNER'S OPERANT BEHAVIOURISM

Many of the important answers we make to daily life are examples of practical behavior, such as reading, writing, driving, and eating. The working environment includes the type of learning in which behavior is most influenced by the consequences that follow. If the environmental changes brought about by behavior are reinforcing — that is, if they offer some reward in nature or eliminate objections — chances are that behaviors will recur. If environmental change does not produce or produce counterproductive motives, the likelihood that behavior will recur may be reduced. Good and bad reinforcement, punitive strategies, and extinction, show how the active state in the settings used can be helpful in improving prosocial and flexible behavior. Practical strategies used by behavioral therapists in parental education programs and weight management programs.

The word sebenziwork 'emphasizes the fact that morality works in the environment to produce results. In Pavlov's method the reinforcer is accompanied by a stimulus, and in active behavior it depends on the reaction. Skinner emphasized the role of nature in shaping and maintaining behavior. The chances of a response increase after positive and negative reinforcement. Good reinforcement involves introducing something, like food, water to the situation. Wrong reinforcement involves removing something, such as a bright light or an electric shock in a situation. The difference between good and bad reinforcement depends on the presence or absence of a given reinforcement that increases the chances of a response. Withdrawal of positive reinforcer has the same effect as the introduction of a negative reinforcement.

Reinforcement results vary based on reinforcement schedules - when and how they are presented.

Non-stop consolidation schedules are:

1. Continuous reinforcement when every output is confirmed

2. Disappearance, when there are no confirmed answers

Occasional consolidation schedules include:

1. A set interval, in which the initial response that occurs after a given period is confirmed, and another period that begins immediately after confirmation.

2. Adjusted rate, in which all nth response is strengthened

3. Flexible interval, in which consolidation is arranged according to a random series of intervals with a given meaning and lying between negative values.

4. A variable rate, in which reinforcement is arranged according to a random series of measurements that have a given meaning and lie between negative values.

5. In general, where one principle of reinforcement applies before one recommendation and a different principle before another recommendation.

6. A different response to the response level, in which the answer is only strengthened if it follows the previous answer after the specified time interval or before the end of the given interval.

The working environment is focused on both the acquisition and retention of behavior. Behavior continues to have consequences, and if these effects or reinforcement do not come when the extinction occurs. Behavior can be shaped by emphasizing consistent sequence to the desired response. When the positive effect of one motivation spreads to other motivations, the result becomes normal.

WOLPE'S RECIPROCAL INHIBITION

Reciprocal inhibition is a form of behavioral therapy in which the desired behavioral response is repeated before the motivation that often triggers an undesirable response. For example, a client who is afraid of snakes may be exposed in the presence of a snake, while practicing a relaxation process. The theory of this type of reciprocal inhibition therapy is that, with sufficient repetition, the old, undesirable response can be learned, and a new behavior pattern can be established permanently.

Reciprocal inhibition has produced a variety of treatments, including treatment for allergies, vaccination therapy, and preventative measures. The first theory of reciprocal inhibition psychotherapy was developed by South African psychologist Joseph Wolpe, who published his ideas in 1958 in a paper entitled Psychotherapy by Reciprocal Inhibition. as well as emotional disturbances by teaching clients to relax during the process of gradual exposure to stimuli that produces anxiety.

Wolpe first demonstrated this concept in a series of cat experiments. The first step in this process was to expose the cats to an unpleasant shock, accompanied by a certain noise. After the suspension, the cats reacted with fear of the noise alone. This is an example of ancient Pavlovian conditioning. Next, Wolpe pointed out that the response to fear may not be read slowly, if it reverses the motivation, and combines the same sound with the presentation of food.

In the theory of reciprocal inhibition, repetitive behavior is defined as competing behavior alone. For example, a comfortable behavior in which the skeletal muscles are relaxed is considered to be the same —stack or fly ‖ response to stress when the muscles tighten. By repeatedly practicing the behavior you want before the stimulus that used to initiate unwanted behavior, the regenerative response diminishes and eventually, if treatment is successful, unwanted behavior is eliminated.

Wolpe developed his ideas by working with soldiers who suffered from post-traumatic stress disorder, and he achieved great success. Initially, the majority of the psychotherapeutic community were skeptical about the theory of reciprocal inhibition, suggesting that this approach would only result in the replacement of symptoms in a patient, not permanent treatment. Wolpe's work, however, created the first psychotherapeutical theory to be closely linked with modern behavioral medicine.

EYSENCK'S INCUBATION THEORY

Eysenck noted that emotional behavior, a distinct feature of which is that the behavior followed by negative consequences is not eliminated, and does not follow Skinner's law of enforcement and cannot be adequately defined in Skinnerian terms. Furthermore, consider that Watson's view of neurosis as an emotional response to the past has not been explained in detail.

Eysenck acknowledged four sources of fear / anxiety response. First, they may have been born. Second, they may refer to 'readiness', which should be read by people. Third, fear can be learned by modeling (imitation). Fourth, and the most important source of learning the answers to fear, classical or Pavlovian conditioning. The main unconditioned stimulus (UCS) that triggers a reaction to the fear of frustration or 'non-rewarding frustration', which can have similar physical and behavioral effects such as pain.

Eysenck is slowly proposing his theory of incubation of neurosis, in hopes of promoting a more relevant clinical and research day collection. Although CS presentation alone always causes a decrease in CR strength, it may also cause an increase. There are therefore two possible effects of CS presentation only. The first is the disappearance of CR, and the other is the development of CR or the insertion of anxiety / fear responses. Evaporation occurs when the decrease exceeds the increasing trend, while the incubation occurs when the increase exceeds the declining trend. There are two categories of CR: those with driving conditions and those without, the first leading to development and those leading to extinction. The CR that leads to extinction, when CS alone is introduced, is the dog's saliva shed, as soaking of saliva does not produce starvation. However, giving mice a shock after a CS presentation only produces a drive made by CS, or a enhancement, and mice will learn new tasks and get used to being stable.

Eysenck suggested that fear / anxiety is a driver-driven response and that is why it is not just about extinction by improving CS presentation. By definition, the first position that UCS produces is fear / anxiety, while CS does not. Combining UCS with CS leads to a situation where, after setting the situation the introduction of CS alone produces a CR of fear / anxiety similar to UCR. It is the CR drive features that make it work similar to UCR, so it provides CS-only presentation enhancement. So when CR for example fear / anxiety, has driving symptoms, the introduction of a CS-only motivation produces CR (improvement). A positive response cycle is established when the fear / anxiety associated with the CS-only presentation itself is a traumatic event, and the motivation associated with CS, with classical conditioning, comes to arouse more fear. This process is not only responsible for the progression but also for the development of neurotic responses.

Incubation has the effect of allowing CR to exceed the power of UCR. In addition, it may cause a gradual increase in neurotic responses over a period of time, with fewer exposure to CS alone. There is ample evidence that the duration of CS presentation time alone is an important factor, with shorter presentations than longer ones that allow for input of fear / anxiety responses. There is little evidence that the strong unlike the weak UCS presentation does that. Eysenck noted that stable extroverts extinguish more easily than other extroversion-neuroticism groups, while neurotic introductions show more evidence of incubation.

The ethical approach to counseling is based on the assumption that the environment determines one's behavior. How a person reacts to a situation is a result of past learning, and often behavior that has been reinforced in the past. For example, suppose a child picks up a spider and sends it to the mother. If he was afraid of spiders, he might shout. The child will then learn that spiders are scared. Next time, instead of picking up the spider, the baby will probably scream and run to its mother, who might say _ooh, I hate spiders, they are so scary ', which reinforces the child's behavior. As a result, the child may develop a fear of spiders and run away from crying (response) when he sees a spider (stimulus). Behavioralists believe that such behavior is 'learned' and therefore can be learned. The basic assumptions of behavior according to the key participants in this approach are described in this chapter.

IX

SLAB III : (EVALUATION AND APPROACHES) TRAINING

Behavioral therapists focus on positive behaviors, current behavioral decisions, learning experiences that promote change, integrating treatment strategies for individual clients, and robust evaluation and evaluation. Behavioral therapy has been used to treat a variety of psychological problems with a variety of clients. Anxiety disorders, depression, drug abuse, eating disorders, domestic violence, sexual problems, pain control, and high blood pressure have all been successfully treated using this method. Behavioral practices are applied in the areas of developmental disability, mental illness, education and special education, community psychology, clinical psychology, rehabilitation, business, self-management, sports psychology, health-related behaviors, and gerontology.

Behavior had its roots in the 1950's and early 1960's, and it was a major departure from the prevailing psychoanalytic view. The behavior of behavioral therapy differs from other therapies in its application of traditional and practical principles in the treatment of a variety of behavioral disorders. In the early 2000's, the "third wave" of moral culture emerged, expanding the scope of research and practice. These new developments include dialectical behavioral therapy, stress-based treatment, psychiatric-based therapy, and acceptance and commitment therapy.

ADVISING TERMS

Six important aspects of behavioral therapy are described below.

1. Behavioral therapy is based on the principles and procedures of the scientific method. Principles of assessment-based learning are systematically used to help people change their misbehavior. The distinguishing feature of ethical workers is their systematic adherence to the accuracy and evaluation of equipment. Behavioral therapists state treatment terms in terms of specific objectives to make the duplication of their interventions possible. Terms of treatment are agreed upon by the client and the therapist. Throughout the course of treatment, the therapist examines the behavior of the problems and the conditions they maintain. Research methods are used to evaluate the effectiveness of both diagnostic and therapeutic procedures. In short, ethical concepts and procedures are explicitly stated, strongly tested, and continuously reviewed.

2. Behavioral therapy addresses current client problems and influential factors, as opposed to the analysis of possible historical decisions. Emphasis is placed on specific factors that influence current performance and what factors can be used to improve performance. Sometimes understanding the past can provide useful information about natural phenomena related to current behavior. Behavioral therapists look at current environmental events that maintain behavioral problems and help clients produce behavioral changes by altering natural phenomena, through a process called functional assessment, or what Wolpe (1990) refers to ukuziphathaa behavior analysis.

3. Clients involved in behavioral therapy are expected to play an active role by engaging in specific actions to address their problems. Rather than simply talking about their condition, they need to take action to bring about change. Clients monitor their behavior during and outside the treatment session, learn and practice coping skills, and imitate a new behavior. Medical activities performed by clients in daily life, or household chores, are an integral part of this approach. Behavioral therapy is a practical and educational approach, and learning is seen as the core of therapy. Clients learn new and flexible behaviors to replace old and inappropriate behaviors.

4. This approach assumes that change is possible without an understanding of basic dynamics. Behavioral therapists work on the basis that behavioral changes can occur before or simultaneously with personal understanding, and that behavioral changes may lead to a growing level of self-awareness. While it is true that understanding and understanding about opportunities that make problems worse can inspire change, knowing that someone has a problem and knowing how to change it are two different things.

5. The focus is on examining explicit and implicit behaviors, identifying the problem, and evaluating change. There is a direct diagnosis of a specific problem by looking at yourself or looking at yourself. Therapists also assess their clients' culture as part of their social environment, which includes social support networks related to targeted behavior. Central to ethical behavior is careful evaluation and intervention testing used to determine whether behavioral change has been the result of a process.

6. Behavioral treatment interventions are individually tailored to specific issues that clients face. Many therapies can be used to treat each client's problems. An important question that serves as a guide for this choice is: "What treatment, by whom, is it most effective for the person with the condition and under what circumstances? ‖

Vaccines play an important role in behavioral therapy. The general purpose of behavioral therapy is to enhance personal choice and create new learning environments. The client, with the help of a therapist, explains certain treatment terms at the beginning of the treatment process. Although screening and treatment occur together, formal testing occurs prior to treatment to determine behavioral goals for change. Continuous evaluation of all treatments determines the extent to which targeted goals are achieved. It is important to establish a method of measuring progress towards goals based on instrument validation.

Modern behavioral therapy emphasizes the active role of clients in determining their treatment. The therapist assists clients in making specific measurable goals. Terms should be clear, concise, understandable, and agreed upon by the client and the consultant. The counselor and client discuss the behaviors associated with the goals, the conditions required for change, the type of sub-conditions, and the action plan to apply these principles. This process of determining treatment goals involves negotiating between the client and the counselor leading to a contract directing the course of treatment. Behavioral therapists and clients change policies throughout the treatment process as needed.

BEHAVIOURAL VALUATIONS

Behavioral therapists perform a comprehensive performance evaluation (or behavioral analysis) to identify endpoints by systematically collecting information about the origin of the condition, the severity of the problem, and the outcome of the problem. This is known as the ABC model, which deals with precursors, behaviors, and outcomes. This behavior model suggests that behavior (B) is influenced by certain pre-existing events, called pre-existing (A), and certain subsequent events called outcomes (C). Previous events are those that indicate or evoke certain behaviors. For example, with a client with a sleep disorder, listening to a rest tape may be an indication of sleep intake. Turning off the lights and removing the TV from the room can also trigger sleep patterns. Consequences are events that maintain treatment in some way by increasing or decreasing it. For example, a client may be more likely to return to counseling after the counselor has given oral praise or encouragement by entering or completing a particular homework assignment. The client may be less likely to return after the counselor arrives late from time to time. In conducting a diagnostic interview, the therapist's job is to identify specific pre- and sequential events that influence or relate to individual performance.

Behavioral-focused employees often work and direct and act as intermediaries and problem solvers. They pay close attention to the instructions given to clients, and are willing to follow their clinical strategies. They use some common techniques in other ways, such as summarizing, reflecting, clarifying, and open-ended questions. However, behavioral doctors also do other work:

· Based on a comprehensive performance appraisal, the counselor makes initial treatment goals and designs and implements a treatment plan to achieve these goals.

· A behavioral therapist uses research-based techniques to be used for a specific type of problem. These strategies are used to encourage normalization and maintenance of behavioral change.

· The clinician evaluates the effectiveness of the change program by measuring progress towards achieving goals throughout the treatment period. Outcome measures are given to the patient at the beginning of treatment (so-called baseline) and recurred periodically during and after treatment to determine if the treatment strategy and plan is effective. If not, changes are being made to the strategies used.

· The primary function of the therapist is to perform follow-up tests to see if the changes are stable over time. Clients learn to identify and deal with potential challenges. Emphasis is placed on helping clients keep track of changes over time and acquiring behavioral and cognitive skills to avoid duplication.

Let's take a look at how a behavioral therapist can perform these tasks. The client comes to treatment to reduce their anxiety, which prevents them from leaving the house. The therapist may begin by analyzing some of his or her concerns. The therapist will ask how she copes with the anxiety of leaving her home, which includes what she actually does in these situations. Systematically, the therapist collects information about this concern. When did the problem start? From what sources? What do you do at these times? What are her feelings and thoughts in these situations? Who is there to deal with anxiety? What is she doing to alleviate her anxiety? How does her present fear affect her life? Following this assessment, certain ethical principles will be developed, and strategies such as relaxation training, planned emotional therapy, and exposure treatment will be designed to help the client reduce their anxiety to a manageable level. The therapist will receive a commitment from her to work on the stated goals, and both will monitor her progress in achieving these goals during treatment.

REST PROCEDURES

Relaxation training is aimed at achieving muscle and mental relaxation and is easily learned. Jacobson (1938) is credited with initiating the process of continuous relaxation. It has since been refined and refined, and relaxation procedures are often used in accordance with this value

other ethical strategies. These include thought-provoking sensitivity processes, structured resistance, vaccination, training, self-regulation programs, tape-recorded instructions, biofeedback-induced relaxation, hypnosis, meditation, and autogenic training training of physical and visual functions through autosuggestion.

Relaxation training involves a few sections that require four to eight hours of instruction. Clients are given a set of instructions asking them to relax. They take the muscles that do nothing and relax. Deep and normal breathing is also associated with producing rest. At the same time, clients are learning to "stop walking" mentally, perhaps by focusing on pleasant thoughts or images. Rest is a well-read-out response, which can be a normal pattern for 20 or 25 minutes daily. During this exercise it helps clients to really feel and feel their strength to see their muscles tighten and learn this tension, and to grip and feel fully the tension. Also, it helps to feel the difference between the season and the relaxed atmosphere.

Until a few years ago relaxation training was used primarily as part of systematic procedures for removing sensitivity. Recently, relaxation procedures have been used in a variety of clinical settings, either as an alternative or in conjunction with related methods. The most common use has complications related to depression and anxiety, which are often manifested by psychosomatic symptoms. Other diseases that you help train to relax include high blood pressure and other cardiovascular problems, headaches, asthma and insomnia.

SYSTEMATIC DESENSITIZATION

Organized resistance, based on the principle of classical conditioning, is a basic ethical framework developed by Joseph Wolpe, one of the pioneers of behavioral therapy. Clients consider situations that cause more anxiety respectively at the same time when engaging in competitive behavior and anxiety. Gradually, or systematically, clients become less sensitive (less sensitive) to a stressful situation. This procedure can be considered as a treatment for exposure because clients need to expose themselves to images that evoke anxiety as a way to reduce anxiety.

Systematic deensitization is a well-researched and time-consuming treatment, yet it is clearly an effective and efficient treatment for anxiety-related problems, especially in the area of specific phobias. Before performing a sensitivity removal procedure, the doctor performs a preliminary interview to identify specific information about the concern and to gather relevant basic information about the client. This interview, which can take a few moments, gives the professional a better understanding of who the client is. The therapist asks the client about specific conditions that cause the condition. For example, under what circumstances does the client feel anxious? If the client is concerned about social issues, does the concern differ with the number of people present? Is the client very concerned about women or men? The client is asked to start a self-assessment process that involves looking at and recording situations during the week that bring about worrying responses. Some therapists also provide a list of questions to gather additional data on conditions that lead to anxiety.

Once a decision has been made to use the desensitization procedure, the doctor gives the client a reason for the procedure and briefly explains what is involved. McNeil and Kyle (2009) describe a number of steps in the application of formal resistance: (1) relaxation training, (2) the development of the anxiety phase, and (3) eliminating systematic sensitivity in a positive way.

Relaxation training steps are presented to the client. The therapist uses a very quiet, soft, and pleasant voice to teach continuous muscle relaxation. The client is asked to create an image of previously relaxed situations, such as sitting by the pool or wandering in a beautiful garden. It is important for the client to achieve a state of calm and tranquility. The client is instructed to practice both as part of the emptiness removal process and outside of the daily session.

The therapist then works with the client to create a stress category for each identified area. The motives that cause concern in a particular place, such as rejection, jealousy, criticism, disapproval, and any other fears, are analyzed. The therapist creates a limited list of conditions that trigger increasing levels of anxiety or avoidance. Positioning arrangements are arranged sequentially from the worst case scenario a client can imagine to a situation that raises the slightest concern. If it is determined that the client has concerns related to fear of rejection, for example, the highest level of productivity concerns may be rejection by a spouse, next, rejection by a close friend, and then rejection by a co-worker. The less disturbing situation can be the negligence of a stranger about a client at a party.

Deleting the sensitivity does not start until a few times after the end of the initial conversation. Sufficient time is allowed for clients to learn to relax during treatment, exercise at home, and build up their anxiety level. The sensitivity removal process begins with the client achieving complete rest with the eyes closed. A neutral forum is presented, and the client is asked to consider it. If the client remains comfortable, please consider a minor situation that raises concerns about the improved case plan. The therapist slowly rises to the skin until the client indicates that he or she is experiencing anxiety, at which point the incident is resolved. The rest is seduced again, and the incident is repeated until a little anxiety is found in it. Treatment is only when the client is able to stay relaxed while contemplating an earlier event that has been very stressful and stressful. The root of systematic resistance is repeated exposure to the imagination in stressful situations without experiencing negative consequences.

Homework and tracking are important factors in eliminating effective sensitivity. Clients can practice selected daily relaxation procedures, at the same time visualizing scenes completed in the previous session. Gradually, they also expose themselves to the elements of daily life as one way to control their anxieties. Clients who often benefit the most when they have a variety of stress management strategies they can continue to use once treatment is over.

Systematic desensitization is an effective treatment for phobias, but it is a misconception that it can only be used to treat anxiety. It is also used to treat a variety of conditions without anxiety, including anger, asthma, insomnia, motion sickness, nightmares, and walking. arousing conditions. The protection is that clients control the process by moving at their own pace and cutting off exposure when they begin to experience more anxiety than they want to tolerate.

BEHAVIOUR REHEARSAL AND ASSERTIVE TRAINING

Behaviour Rehearsal

Community skills training is a broad phase that deals with one's ability to interact effectively with others in a variety of social situations; used to address shortcomings in clients' ability to communicate. Communication skills include the ability to communicate effectively and effectively. People who experience psychological and social problems caused by hardship among people are good

who will be trained in community skills. One of the desirable features of this training is that it has a very broad working base and can be easily customized to suit the specific needs of individual customers. Social skills training includes psychological teaching, modeling, reinforcement, behavioral practice, role play, and feedback. Another popular form of social skills training is anger management training, designed for people with a problem with aggressive behavior. Vaccination training, described below, is for people who do not have immunization skills.

Assertive Training

Another special type of community skills training that has gained popularity is to teach people how to excel in various social situations. Many people feel that it is right or wrong to take action. People who lack good communication skills often have to deal with problems at home, at work, in school, and during leisure time. Vigorous training can be helpful to those who (1) have a hard time expressing their anger or frustration, (2) have a hard time saying no, (3) are extremely modest and allow others to take advantage of it, and (4) find it difficult. to express love and other positive reactions, (5) those who feel they have no right to express their thoughts, beliefs, or feelings, or (6) who have a fear of the community.

The basic premise of vaccination training is that people have a right (but not an obligation) to express themselves. One goal of immunization training is to extend the ethical profile of individuals so that they can choose whether to act responsibly in certain situations. It is important for customers to replace negative social skills with new skills. Another goal is to teach people to express their feelings in ways that show empathy for the feelings and rights of others. Vaccination does not mean anger; people who are truly assertive do not always defend their rights, ignoring the feelings of others.

Vaccination training is based on the principles of community learning theory and includes a wide range of community skills training methods. Usually, both therapists teach and demonstrate the desired behavior the client seeks. These behaviors are practiced in the medical office and are practiced in everyday life. Many vaccination training programs focus on customer malpractice, self-defeating beliefs, and misconceptions. People tend to behave in an unethical way because they do not think they have the right to express their opinion or to ask for what they want or deserve. So their thinking leads to a life of idleness. Effective training programs do more than provide people with the skills and strategies to deal with difficult situations. These programs challenge people's beliefs associated with their lack of assertiveness and teach them to make constructive statements and adopt a new set of beliefs that will lead to assertive behavior.

Vaccination training is usually done in groups. Using the group format, modeling and instructions are presented to the whole group, and members are trained in behavioral skills in role-playing situations. After practice, the member is given a response that includes reinforcing appropriate behavioral features and guidelines for how to improve behavior. Each member participates in further training of assertive behavior until the skills are developed adequately in different contexts.

Because authentication training is based on Western assumptions of the value of the vaccine, it may not be appropriate for clients with a cultural background that emphasizes consistency rather than assertiveness. This approach can be an effective treatment for clients who lack skills in assertive behavior or for people who are experiencing difficulties in their relationships with other people. While counselors may not be able to adapt these types of community skills training processes to suit their style, it is important to include behavioral repetition and continuous assessment as key elements of the program.

REINFORCEMENT METHODS

This section outlines a few important principles of working conditions: positive reinforcement, negative reinforcement, extinction, positive punishment, and negative punishment.

In the behavioral analysis used, situation performance techniques and methods of assessment and evaluation are used for a variety of problems in many different settings. The most important contribution of the ethical analysis used is that it provides an effective way to understand customer problems and deal with these issues through preliminary changes and outcomes (ABC model).

Behavioralists believe that we respond in unpredictable ways because of the benefits we receive (positive reinforcement) or because of the need to avoid or avoid negative consequences (negative reinforcement). Once customer values have been tested, special behavior is directed. The goal of reinforcement, whether positive or negative, is to increase targeted behavior. Good reinforcement involves the addition of something of value to a person (such as praise, attention, money, or food) as a result of certain behaviors. Behavioral motivation is a good reinforcement. For example, a child receives excellent marks and is commended for reading to his parents. If he or she appreciates this recommendation, you may be able to afford a scholarship in the future. If the goal of the program is to reduce or eliminate unwanted behavior, positive reinforcement is often used to increase the frequency of highly desirable behaviors, replacing unwanted behaviors.

Negative reinforcement includes escaping or avoiding contradictory (unpleasant) motives. A person is encouraged to show the kind of attitude that he wants to avoid in order to avoid an unpleasant situation. For example, a person who does not enjoy waking up to the sound of a clock has to practice waking up a few minutes before the alarm goes off to avoid alarming.

Another effective way to change behavior is extinction, which refers to capturing reinforcement from a previously reinforced response. In the settings used, disassembly can be used for behavior stored for good reinforcement or for negative reinforcement. For example, in the case of angry children, parents often insist that the behavior be directed to their attention. The way to deal with problematic behavior is to eliminate the connection between certain behaviors (irritability) and positive reinforcement (attention). Doing so can minimize or eliminate such behaviors as a result of the extinction process. It should be noted that the disappearance may have negative consequences, such as anger and rage. Extermination may reduce or eliminate certain behaviors, but extinction does not replace those already deleted responses. For this reason, extinction is often used in behavioral rehabilitation programs in line with various strengthening strategies.

One way behavior is controlled is punishment, sometimes called controlling behavior, when the consequences of certain behaviors result in a decline in that behavior. The goal of reinforcement is to increase targeted behavior, but the goal of punishment is to reduce targeted behavior. There are two types of punishment that can occur as a result of behavior: good punishment and bad punishment. In good discipline opposing encouragement is added after the behavior to reduce the frequency of behavior (such as withholding a gift for a child due to misconduct or blaming a student for imitating the class). In the case of adverse punishment a strong motivation is removed following behaviors that reduce the frequency of targeted behavior (such as withdrawing money from work due to time off work, or depriving a child of television time for misconduct). In both cases, there is little chance of future behavior. These four working principles form the basis of ethical treatment programs for parenting skills training and are also used in the self-management process.

Skinner (1948) believed that punishment had a limited value in changing behavior and was often an undesirable means of changing behavior. He opposed the use of counter-control or punishment, and recommended that it be substituted for good reinforcement. The main goal in the behavioral analysis method used is to use small methods that may be able to change behavior, and positive reinforcement is known as the most powerful change agent. Skinner believed in the importance of analyzing the natural features of both the causes and remedies for behavioral problems and argued that the greatest benefits to the individual and the community occurred through positive formal reinforcement as a means of behavioral control.

In everyday life, punishment is often used as a form of revenge or frustration. However, the punishment in everyday life will not be able to teach lessons or force intolerable behavior because of certain punishments used and the way they are used. Even in those cases where discipline is not a factor, the punishment does not lead to the teaching of desirable behavior. Punishment should be applied only after non-withdrawal methods have been used and found to be ineffective in changing the problematic behavior. It is important that reinforcement is used as a means of promoting positive behavior instead of oppressed behavior.

Behavioral therapy differs respectfully not only from basic concepts but also from techniques that can be used to deal with specific problems in a variety of clients. Behavioral movement involves four areas of development: classical conditioning, operant conditioning, social learning theory, and increasing attention to the psychological factors that influence behavior. A unique feature of behavioral therapy is its strong reliance on.

Limitations and Criticisms of Behavior Therapy

Behavioral therapy has been criticized for a variety of reasons. Common criticisms and misconceptions people often have about behavioral therapy are: (i) Behavioral therapy may change behavior, but it does not change emotions. Some critics argue that emotions must change before behaviors can change. A common criticism of both ethics and understanding is that clients are not encouraged to have their own feelings.

(ii) Behavioral therapy ignores important aspects of relationships in therapy. Charges are often made so that the value of the relationship between the client and the therapist is reduced in behavioral therapy. (iii) Behavioral therapy does not provide understanding. If this assertion is true, ethical therapists would probably say that understanding is not a requirement for changing behavior. However, a change in behavior often leads to a change in attitude or understanding, and often leads to emotional changes. (iv) Behavioral therapy for symptoms has causes. Behavioral therapists may admit that erroneous answers have historical origins, but they argue that history is rarely important in caring for current problems. However, behavioral therapists emphasize the changing nature of the current environment in order to change behavior. (v) Behavioral therapy involves the control and exploitation of a therapist. All therapists have a power relationship with the client and thus have control over it. Of course, in every treatment there is the control of a therapist, who hopes to change the behavior in some way. However, this does not mean that clients are helpless victims with the kindness and standards of the therapist. Modern behavioral therapists use techniques aimed at increasing self-regulation and self-improvement, which are clients of skills who are actually learning the healing process.

X

COGNITIVE BEHAVIOUR THERAPY

Cognitive Behavior Therapy (CBT) is a form of psychotherapy that focuses on examining the relationships between thoughts, feelings, and behavior. By examining thought patterns that lead to self-harm and the beliefs that guide these thoughts, clients can change their thinking patterns to improve coping. Refers to a intervention group that shares the view that depression is supported by cognitive factors. Pioneered by Ellis (1962) and Beck (1970), a CBT principle that negative thoughts promote the development of depression and behavioral difficulties. These negative thoughts incorporate a person's common beliefs about himself, the world, and the future (Beck, 1970), creating spontaneous thoughts that may be erroneous, wrong, or unhelpful in certain situations.

The concept of psychotherapy is that the way you think determines how you feel and act. CBT as a treatment focuses on the basic premise that misbehavior arises from human error, which can be caused by pressures from the individual, the environment, and / or others. The basic premise of CBT is that emotions are difficult to change directly, so CBT directs emotions by changing thoughts and behaviors that contribute to stressful emotions. Using an evidence-based approach, CBT is a short-term psychotherapy, currently focused on helping people change negative thinking and behavior, as a way to help solve current problems (Beck, 1967)

TECHNIQUES

Psychiatrists use both ethical and psychological strategies to develop new therapies tailored to the needs of the client. There are many different CBT methods and techniques that can be combined to work as one. All strategies cover a key part of the mental reorganization as developed by Ellis and Beck. Below is a list of strategies that can be included in treatment:

Stress Inoculation Training (SIT): A three-stage stress reduction method; thinking skills, acquisition skills and practice, use and follow-up. This approach assumes that if people are able to cope with less stress, they will be able to cope and cope more effectively with the most difficult ones. Treatment usually consists of a 12-15 weekly session and an additional follow-up session within 6-12 months.

Behavioral Activation Therapy (BAT): Involves a growing daily activity to help motivate people with depression who may be low in energy and who may have withdrawn from life. BAT is often introduced at the beginning of antidepressant treatment, to help people increase their levels of activity, improve their mood, and provide a source of happiness on which to build. Strategies used include creating a list of fun activities, planning, monitoring, and marital activities; rest and skills training; recognizing contemptuous and avoidable behavior; and dealing with mental disorders.

Behavior Training (HAT): Uses reinforcement and other behaviors strategies to help people recognize the signs of past behavior occur, monitor their behavior during stressful situations, use strategies for relaxing, and practicing other incompatible behaviors morally they are trying to extinguish it. Exposure: Exposure is one of the most important parts of understanding or cognitive-behavioral therapy for anxiety disorders. Through exposure, one learns to identify one's responses to fear; see poor eyesight, dealing with uncomfortable feelings without avoidance, escape or change experience; and gain somethingthe amount of being able to do it yourself or to control feelings of depression. Strategies such as the Flood, the exposure of the titles, and the general intolerance different types of exposure-based therapies.

Eye Movement Insensitivity and Rethinking (EMDR): Method of exposure therapy that combines dual revitalization (eye movement, sound exchange, and tapping), behavioral conflicts, and comprehension rearrangement in a systematic eight-phase program. EMDR applies to treatment of anxiety and mood disorders, certain phobias, diet and behavior chaos.

Problem Solving Therapy (PST): Consists of a four step process: Problem identification, alternatives, cost / profit making analysis of possible solutions, and monitoring and evaluating outcomes. With PST, clients reduce critical decisions, reduce conflict, and reducing the use of maladaptive coping skills such as avoidance, inaction, or emotional disturbances. Visualization can be used to help clients think to achieve the goal successfully.

ALBERT ELLIS'S RATIONAL EMOTIVE BEHAVIOUR THERAPY

Rational Emotive Behavior therapy (REBT) was one of the first psychiatric treatments, and it continues to be a major psychological treatment. The basic premise of REBT is that people contribute to their psychological problems, as well as certain symptoms, by the way they describe events and situations. REBT is based on the idea that perception, emotion, and behavior are highly interdependent and have a causal and causal relationship. REBT has consistently emphasized all three of these approaches and their interoperability, thus qualifying as an integrated approach.

REBT not only believes that the way we think affects our emotions and behavior, it also tries to help clients change their mindset in order to reduce negative symptoms and improve their quality of life.

"People are not distracted by things but their ideas." - Albert Ellis

Rational Emotive Behavior Therapy assumes that many people with emotional or behavioral problems struggle because of the way they see their experiences instead of just seeing them for themselves. REBT aims to facilitate changes in contextual beliefs and thought patterns that will enable customers to more effectively deal with their problems and improve their ability to work and feel healthier.

According to Ellis the psychoanalytic method sometimes does not work well because people often appear to be worse off instead of better. He began to encourage his clients to do the very things he feared most to do, such as risking the loss of important people. Although REBT is generally accepted as the parent of modern morality, Greek philosophy, in particular, Stoicism has influenced Ellis' view. Epictetus, who said 2,000 years ago: "People are not disturbed by events, but by the ideas they take from them". Ellis argues that human self-esteem is broader and more accurate: —People are distracted by their own experiences, thoughts, feelings, and actions‖.

Ellis also credits Adler as an influential figure. Adler believed that our emotional response to life was linked to our basic beliefs and therefore to reason. Like the Adlerian approach, REBT emphasizes the role of public interest in determining mental health. There are other Adlerian influences on REBT, such as the importance of goals, objectives, values, and meanings in a person's life.

Ellis believed that approaching our problems in a positive way could have a profound effect on our negative emotions and misbehavior. The most important challenge we must face on the road to wisdom is our flawed or irrational thinking.

Ellis was of the opinion that many of our emotional and moral problems arise from baseless logic or preconceived notions and that they influence people to act in ways that are wrong, helpless, or harmful. and behavior.

The ABCDE Model of Emotional Disturbance

Ellis thought that irrational beliefs were the result of restricted or imposed human goals or desires. If we do not get what we want or if we do not get what we want, we may have superstitious beliefs about ourselves or the world around us.

For example, imagine that you are very eager to get the job you are applying for. You study in the company, practice the answers to your interview, and make sure you look very sharp on the day of the interview. Despite much preparation, the hiring manager decided to go with another candidate.

You may agree that this was not intended to be so, or that you were not qualified for the job. However, you may be deeply moved by the decision and develop an unreasonable belief in why you did not get the job.

You may think, I did not get this job because they see that I am cruel. I'm not good at anything and I won't be. "

Or, you may think, —One reason I could not get this job was because the hiring manager had done it for me. It's as if the whole universe has reserved for me! "

Both of these ideas can help you explain why you did not get a job, but they are irrational and can lead to negative feelings and behavior.

To use this situation as an example, here is how the ABCDE model can explain the development (and solution) of such problems:

A - *Starting Event / Difficulty*

Tricky or difficult event is something that causes you to create an absurd belief, such as a denial of position. It is a first step in developing an imaginary mind because an irrational thought is created to help you deal with an event.

B - *Ignorant Belief*

The word —B‖ represents an absurd belief formed in response to a sensitive event. This is a belief that you use to deal with an event, such as —I'm lost, I have no job, and I will not be able to do the job anyway.‖ Although this, of course, is extremely harmful. i think, it can still be more comforting than not knowing why you did not get a job.

C - *The Effects of Emotions and Behavior*

The third part is the consequences of this absurd belief. Unreasonable beliefs always have consequences, sometimes emotional, sometimes moral, and sometimes both. In this case, the consequences may be that you lose your self-confidence or that you often feel sad (emotionally) and stop applying for any (moral) activities.

D - *Disputes or Disputes*

At times, you may realize that you do not have the faith to try to solve problems. You see your loss of self-confidence and negative thoughts about yourself and you begin to challenge your irrational beliefs. If you work with a therapist, a therapist can help guide you in developing arguments against the belief and help you come up with contradictory evidence, such as —I have a wonderful wife (life partner). Women (Spouse) will not be a 'failure' so I must not be a failure.

E - *New Result*

If you have successfully erased your irrational beliefs, you will see new results or results (hopefully better) or results. In our example, these results may boost your confidence, apply for more jobs, and make you feel good about your skills. These results are good for capturing common sense, such as —I'm not qualified for the job, but I will get another‖ or —Perhaps the hired manager really did not like me, but he did. loss‖.

The ABCDE model can be very helpful in pursuing the development of mindless thinking and provides a high-level framework for challenging again and in its place.

REBT's basic hypothesis is that our emotions are deeply rooted in our beliefs, in our analysis, interpretation and response to life situations. Through the healing process, clients learn skills that give them the tools to identify and refute the absurd beliefs they have acquired and built for themselves and are now being held to believe. They learn how to replace unhealthy thinking patterns with practical and logical reasoning, and as a result change their emotional response to situations. The treatment process allows clients to apply the REBT principles of change not only to a specific problem but also to many other life problems or future problems they may face.

Several therapeutic effects flow from these considerations: Focused on thinking and acting rather than expressing emotions. Treatment is considered an educational process. The therapist works in a variety of ways as a teacher, especially in working with the client on homework and in teaching critical thinking techniques; and the client is a student, practicing the skills learned in everyday life.

REBT differs from other early therapies in its focus on the present; in fact, according to Ellis, a common misconception is that the past has a profound effect on our present life. While the past shapes what we are today, it is an absurd belief if you feel that you cannot escape the past.

The goal of Rational Emotive Behavior Therapy is better summarized as —contraditional‖ - to challenge and question our irrational and ineffective beliefs and to replace them with rational and practical beliefs. The result is not just a change in a few thoughts or a reduction in certain symptoms, but a new outlook on life.

REBT also differs from many other therapies in that it does not place great importance on casual association, working with dreams, focusing on a client's past history, expressing and evaluating emotions, or dealing with referral situations. Although transfers and contradictions may occur spontaneously in therapy, Ellis (2008) stated that —laus is quickly analyzed, the philosophies behind you are exposed, and often evaporate in this process‖. In addition, when a client's deepest feelings arise, the client is not given much opportunity to sink in or take over. Ellis believes that such cathartic work may make clients feel better, but it will not help them get better.

AARON BECK'S COGNITIVE THERAPY

Aaron Beck (1921-) is regarded as the father of psychotherapy, having developed a technique known as cognitive therapy (CT) as a result of his research on depression. Beck developed psychotherapy in the belief that human experience triggers perceptions or thoughts. This understanding is linked to schemes, which are fundamental beliefs formed from an early age, in order to shape our view of the world and to determine our emotional and moral state. Beck believes the chaos is fueled by negative attitudes and distorted thinking. Beck was designing his psychiatric treatment at about the same time Ellis did REBT, yet both seemed to be creating their own ways independently. Beck's study of depressed clients revealed that they had a negative bias in their interpretation of certain life events, which contributed to their mental turmoil. Psychotherapy has many similarities in both rational behavioral therapy and behavioral therapy. All of these therapies are effective, instructive, timed, problem-oriented, interdependent, organized, effective, using homework, and require a clear identification of the problems and conditions in which they occur.

Psychotherapy identifies psychological problems as arising from common practices such as misconceptions, misconceptions on the basis of incorrect or incorrect information, and failure to distinguish between myth and fact. Like REBT, CT is a cognitive-based treatment that emphasizes the recognition and transformation of negative and maladaptive thoughts.

beliefs. Therefore, the model of therapeutic psychological education. Psychotherapy is based on the theory that how people feel and behave is determined by how they perceive and organize their knowledge. The hypothetical hypotheses of psychiatry are (1) that internal communication is accessible to self-assessment, (2) that client beliefs have more personal meaning, and (3) that these definitions can be found by the client rather than taught. or translated by a therapist.

Psychiatry was originally designed to treat depression and later expanded to treat other mental health problems including anxiety, anorexia, bulimia, sexual dysfunction, physical disorders, post-traumatic stress disorder, and substance abuse. It has been found to be useful as a temporary treatment and a long-term treatment model for adults, children, adolescents, and groups.

Psychiatry is based on the belief that what we think affects the way we feel, behave, and react to our environment. In fact, research shows that our emotional problems can be traced back to our beliefs about our experiences. The goal of psychotherapy is to identify and change our distorted or negative beliefs in order to improve our morals and lives. Psychiatrists believe that distorted client thinking about them, the world, and the future is a major cause of their stressful experiences as shown in the picture below.

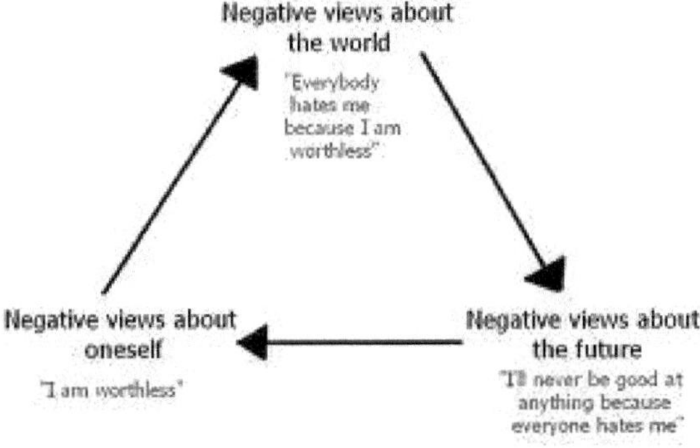

Eexperiences of depression

In psychotherapy, clients learn about the connection between their emotional responses and spontaneous thoughts, which is a deeper understanding; schemes, and mental distortions, biased thinking. For example, the thought of 'I am nothing' may make you sad.

The basic theory of CT states that in order to understand the nature of a traumatic event or disorder it is important to focus on the mental content of a person's reaction to an annoying event or series of thoughts. The goal is to change the way clients think by using their default ideas to reach the main schemata and begin to present the idea of schema redesign. This is done by encouraging clients to gather and analyze the evidence supporting their beliefs.

Basic Principles of Cognitive Therapy

Beck, a psychoanalytic specialist for many years, became interested in the automatic thoughts of his clients (personal opinions caused by certain motives that lead to emotional response). As part of her psychoanalytic research, she explored the content of dreams for clients who were depressed because of the anger she was taking for herself. He began to realize that instead of turning his back on anger, as Freud described the depression, clients were displaying a biased attitude toward their interpretation or thinking. Beck urged clients to look for persistent negative thoughts that persist despite contradicting objective evidence, and in this case he created a broad theory of depression.

Beck argues that people with emotional difficulties often make traits of —m logical mistakes‖ that lead to a blurring of true goal and make a person feel inferior. Listed below are some systematic errors in thinking that lead to wrong thinking and erroneous ideas, called mental distortions.

· Misconceptions refer to making conclusions without supporting and important evidence. This includes wenzamaking disaster, ‖ or thinking about the worst case scenario and the consequences of many situations. You can start your first career by making sure you will not be liked or informed about your colleagues or clients. You are sure that you cheated on your professors and somehow managed to get your degree, but now people will know for sure who you are.

· Selected citations include making conclusions based on individual event details. In this process some information is disregarded, and the value of the context is lost. It is thought that the most important events are those that deal with failure and deprivation. As a new employee, you may measure your value by your faults and weaknesses, not by your success.

· Normal extremism is the process of capturing extremist beliefs on the basis of a single incident and misusing them in different events or settings. If you have difficulty working with one aspect of the job, for example, if you work as a counselor because of the difficulty of working with one child you may conclude that you will not have effective advice for any young people. You can too

we conclude that you will not work successfully with any clients.

• Increasing and minimizing involves seeing a case or situation with greater or lesser light than we really should. You can make this misunderstanding by assuming that even small mistakes in counseling a client can cause problems for the individual and can lead to psychological damage.

• Self-efficacy is the practice of individuals relating external events to themselves, even if there is no reason to make such a connection.
If the client does not return for a second counseling session, you may be absolutely sure that this absence is due to your poor performance during the first session. You may tell yourself, —This situation proves that I have really disappointed that client, and now she may not need help again.

• Labeling and lying involves revealing one's identity on the basis of imperfection and mistakes made in the past and allowing oneself to be exposed. So, if you can not meet all the expectations of the client, you may tell yourself, "I'm nothing at all and I should stop practicing immediately."

• Different thinking involves classifying the experience into categories or extremes. With such polarized thinking, events are written in black or white words. You may have the opportunity to be imperfect and to be imperfect counselors. You may consider yourself a fully competent mentor (meaning always successful with all clients) or as a total flop if you can fully (which means there is no room for any mistakes).

The Core Ideas of Cognitive Therapy

• Psychiatric therapy is based on the discovery that changes in thought lead to changes in mood and behavior.

• Treatment requires a sound and co-operative treatment alliance.

• Treatment is usually short-lived, problem-oriented, and goal-oriented.

• Psychiatric therapy is an effective and systematic treatment.

• Focuses on the present, although past attention when indicated.

• Careful diagnosis, diagnosis, and treatment planning are essential.

• Psychiatry uses a variety of techniques and interventions to help people analyze and change their perceptions.

• Educational thinking and Socialist questions are very important strategies.

• This is a psychoeducational model that improves emotional health and prevents recurrence by teaching people to identify, evaluate, and change their own perceptions.

• Assigned tasks, tracking, and customer feedback are essential to ensure the success of this approach.

A psychologist works by assuming that the correct way to change negative emotions and behavior is to change negative thoughts and actions.

The psychiatrist teaches clients how to identify these distorted and ineffective conditions through a diagnostic procedure. Through collaborative effort, clients learn the influence it has on their emotions and behavior even at environmental events. In psychiatry, clients learn to engage in rational thinking, especially if they are constantly aware of times when they are often caught up in traumatic thinking. Once they have gained an understanding of how their irrational negative thoughts affect them, clients are trained to test these preconceived notions against facts by examining and measuring their evidence and against them. They can begin to monitor the frequency with which these beliefs are introduced into everyday life. The most frequently asked question is, —What evidence is there? ‖ If this question is raised frequently enough, customers may make it a practice to ask themselves this question, especially as they become more skilled at identifying ineffective thoughts. This process of carefully examining their core beliefs involves actively experimenting with actively participating in Socrates' talk with the therapist, doing homework, collecting data about guesswork, keeping a record of activities, and making other explanations. Clients formulate thoughtful ideas about their behavior and eventually learn to use specific problem-solving and coping skills. Through the process of targeted discovery, clients gain insight into the connection between their thinking and the ways they act and feel.

Psychotherapy focuses on current problems, regardless of whether the client is diagnosed. The latter may be incorporated into therapy where the therapist sees it as important to understand how and when certain important ineffective beliefs originated and that these ideas have a current impact on a particular client schema. The objectives of this short course of treatment include providing symptomatic relief, assisting clients in resolving their most pressing issues, and teaching clients strategies for preventing relapse.

OTHER DIFFERENCES BETWEEN CT AND REBT

In both Beck and REBT psychotherapy, physical examination is highly organized. Clients come to the point of experience that they do not fully understand the situations. However there are significant differences between REBT and CT, especially in terms of treatments and style.

REBT is often direct, persuasive, and controversial; it also focuses on the teaching role of the therapist. The therapist shows common sense and helps clients identify and refute unreasonable beliefs. In contrast, CT uses Socratic dialogue by asking open-ended questions to clients with the aim of making clients think about personal issues and reach their conclusions. CT places more emphasis on helping clients discover and identify their own erroneous ideas than REBT. Through this thoughtful questioning process, a psychiatrist tries to work with clients to assess the appropriateness of their knowledge (a process called collaborative empiricism). Therapeutic changes are the result of clients facing errors and contradictory evidence that they have collected and analyzed.

There is also a difference in the way Ellis and Beck view flawed thinking. Through a process of rational controversy, Ellis works to show customers that their particular beliefs are irrational and do not work. Beck (1976) takes away from the REBT concept of irrational beliefs. Psychiatrists view superstitious beliefs as problematic because they interfere with normal mental processing, not because they are irrational. Instead of irrational beliefs, Beck emphasizes that some ideas are more complete, broader, and more extreme. To him, people live by rules (structures or formulas); they get into trouble when they label, interpret, and evaluate a collection of untrue rules or when they misuse or abuse the rules. If clients make a commitment to live by the rules that can lead to unhappiness, the therapist may suggest other rules to consider, without distorting the mind. Although psychotherapy often begins with seeing a client reference framework, the therapist continues to look for evidence of some form of belief system.

DONALD MEICHENBAUM'S COGNITIVE BEHAVIOUR MODIFICATION

Another great alternative to mindfulness therapy is Donald Meichenbaum's cognitive behavior modification (CBM), which focuses on changing the client's response. According to Meichenbaum, self-expression affects a person's behavior in the same way that a person does. The basic premise of CBM is that clients, as a requirement for behavior change, should be aware of how they think, feel, and behave and the impact it has on others. In order for change, clients need to adjust their written behavior in order to be able to assess their behavior in a variety of contexts.

Cognitive-behavioral modification (CBM) is a mental-behavioral therapy technique that focuses on transforming your negative speech and health accounts into positive self-expression. The basis of this treatment is that negative speech can manifest itself in a person's behavior. The goal of CBM is to change a person's story or life story from bad to worse. This is done by focusing on the strength and resilience of the client. CBM also helps clients forgive themselves for wrongdoing in the past and move forward with hope and hope for the future. With a positive change in perspective and life narrative, the actions and behaviors of the client will follow the same.

This approach is associated with REBT and Beck's psychotherapy for the idea that depressive emotions are often the result of negative thoughts. There is a difference, however. While REBT is very straightforward and controversial in revealing and refuting irrational ideas, Meichenbaum's self-discipline training focuses on helping clients become more aware of their own expressions. The treatment process consists of teaching clients to make their own statements and training clients to change the instructions they give them so that they can deal with the problems they face. Together, the therapist and the client practice self-discipline and desirable behavior in role-playing situations that mimic stress situations in the daily life of the client. Emphasis on acquiring practical skills to deal with problematic situations such as impulsive behavior and aggression, fear of experimentation, and fear of public speaking.

Psychological reorganization plays an important role in Meichenbaum's (1977) approach. He describes the formation of the mind as part of the planning process of thought, which seems to monitor and direct the selection of thoughts. Comprehension refers to a ephethe processor in charge, ‖ hethe with a thought plan‖ that determines when to proceed, interrupt, or change thinking.

1 Change in Behavior

Meichenbaum (1977) argues that koku behavioral change occurs in a series of mediation processes that include internal communication, thought structures, and behavior and its resulting consequences‖. Describes the process of three stages of change in which those three components are integrated. According to him, focusing on one aspect will probably not be enough.

Stage 1: Self-examination. The first step in the transformation process consists of clients learning to monitor their behavior. When clients start treatment, their internal dialogue is characterized by negative statements and pictures. An important factor is determination and the ability to listen.

This process involves more sensitivity to their thoughts, feelings, actions, physical reactions, and ways of responding to others. If depressed clients hope to make positive changes, for example, they should first realize that they are not —a victims of negative thoughts and feelings. Rather, they are actually contributing to the depression of the things they tell. Although self-examination is necessary in the event of a change, it is not enough for the change. As treatment progresses, clients discover new thinking structures that allow them to look at their problems in a new way. This rethinking process arises through a collaborative effort between the client and the therapist.

Step 2: Starting a new internal dialogue. As a result of contact with the first client of the client, clients learn to recognize their inappropriate behavior, and begin to see the potential for dynamic behaviors. If clients are hoping to change what they tell themselves, they should start a new series of behaviors, which are not in line with their inappropriate behavior. Clients are learning to change their internal conversation about treatment. Their new internal dialogue serves as a guide for new behaviors. Next, this process has an impact on customer perceptions.

Phase 3: Learning new skills. The third phase of the transformation process consists of teaching clients effective coping skills, which are practiced in real-life situations. (For example, clients who are unable to cope with failure may avoid attractive jobs for fear that they will not succeed. Psychological reorganization may help them change their negative thinking, thus making them more willing to participate in desirable activities.) At the same time. , clients continue to focus on inventing new sentences and looking at and evaluating results. Because they behave differently in situations, they often experience different reactions from others. The stability of what they learn is greatly influenced by what they themselves say about their newly acquired behavior and its consequences.

2 Resilience Skills Programs

The reason for coping skills programs is that we can find effective strategies for dealing with stressful situations by learning how to change our mind — set, ‖ or our core beliefs. The following procedures are designed to teach coping skills:

○ Exposing clients to stressful situations by playing a role and image
○ It requires clients to assess their level of anxiety
○ Educating clients to be aware of the stress-causing understanding they receive in stressful situations
○ Helping clients evaluate these ideas by reviewing their statements
○ Having clients identify the level of anxiety following this review

Studies have shown the effectiveness of problem-solving skills programs when used in problems such as speech anxiety, test anxiety, fear, anger, social dysfunction, addiction, alcoholism, sexual dysfunction, post-traumatic stress disorder in children, and social withdrawal in children.

A specific coping skills program is to teach clients stress management strategies in the form of a strategy known as stress inoculation.

Using cognitive techniques, Meichenbaum has developed injecting psychological and behavioral analog injections into vaccines at the biological level. Individuals are given opportunities to deal with the causes of low stress in effective ways, so that they gradually develop stronger motivations. This training is based on the assumption that we can improve our ability to cope with stress by changing our beliefs and statements about our performance in stressful situations. Meichenbaum's stress injection training is more than just teaching people specific coping skills. His program is designed to prepare clients for interventions and motivate them to change, and it addresses issues such as resistance back. Stress Inoculation (SIT) training includes a combination of informative, Socrates dialogue, mental reorganization, problem solving, relaxation training, behavioral repetition, self-awareness, self-awareness, self-reliance, and environmental change.

conditions. This approach is designed to teach coping skills that can be applied to both current problems and future difficulties. Meichenbaum (2003) argues that SIT can be used for both prevention and treatment purposes for a wide range of people experiencing stress responses.

Meichenbaum has designed a three-phase model of stress vaccine training:

(1) the concept-teaching phase, (2) the acquisition of skills, integration, and the practice phase, and (3) the application and follow-up phase.

During the concept-teaching phase, the main focus is on creating working relationships with clients. This is mainly done by helping them to better understand the nature of stress and to recognize it in terms of social interaction. The therapist incorporates client interaction in this early stage and together they reconsider the nature of the problem. Initially, clients were provided with a conceptual framework with simple words designed to teach them how to deal with various stressful situations.

They learn the role of understanding and emotion in creating and maintaining stress through didactic presentations, Socrates questions, and the process of self-discovery.

Clients often begin treatment with the feeling that they are the victims of external circumstances, thoughts, feelings, and behaviors over which they have control. Training involves teaching clients to recognize their role in creating stress. They get this awareness systematically looking at the statements they make internally and monitoring the misconduct arising from this internal discussion. Such self-examination continues at all stages. Clients usually keep an open diary where they systematically record their specific thoughts, feelings, and behavior. When teaching these coping skills, therapists strive for flexibility in their use of strategies and are sensitive to the individual, cultural, and individual circumstances of their clients.

During the acquisition of skills, integration, and the exercise phase, the focus is on providing clients with a variety of behavioral and cognitive strategies for use in stressful situations. This category includes specific actions, such as collecting information about their fears, learning exactly what stressors are, planning ways to reduce stress by doing something different, and learning ways to relax physically and mentally.

During the application and follow-up phase, the focus is on carefully planning the transfer and maintenance of the transition from treatment to daily life. It is clear that teaching coping skills is a complex process that depends on a variety of treatment options. For clients to simply say new things to themselves is often not enough to produce change. See they need to practice these statements themselves and apply their new skills in real life situations. Combining lessons learned during training sessions, clients participate in a variety of activities, including image repetition and behavior, role play, modeling, and in vivo practice.

When clients have knowledge of cognitive and behavioral skills, they perform ethical assignments, which becomes more difficult. They were asked to write down their homework. The results of these assignments are carefully considered at subsequent meetings, and if clients do not follow them, both the therapist and the client collectively consider the reasons for the failure. Clients are also provided with training on prevention prevention, which includes procedures for dealing with the inevitable challenges they may face as they apply their learning in everyday life. Follow-up sessions with a booster usually take place over a period of 3, 6, and 12 months as an incentive for clients to continue training and refine their coping skills. SIT can be considered part of an ongoing stress management program that expands the benefits of training into the future.

Stress management training has applications that can be helpful for a variety of problems with clients as well as both remediation and prevention. Some of these apps include anger control, anxiety control, self-control, developing critical thinking, treating depression, and dealing with health problems. Depression vaccination training has been employed with medical and psychiatric patients. SIT has been used successfully with children, adolescents, and adults with anger problems; anxiety disorders; and posttraumatic stress disorder (PTSD).

Cognitive Behavioral Therapy (CBT) is a treatment that focuses on examining the relationship between thoughts, feelings, and behavior. By examining thought patterns that lead to self-harm and the beliefs that guide these thoughts, clients can change their thinking patterns to improve coping.

Rational emotive behavior therapy (REBT) focuses on helping clients change irrational beliefs. Ellis‘ goal was to develop a psychosocial approach designed to produce results by helping clients manage their emotions, thoughts, and behavior. Rational Emotive Therapists believe that the way people feel is greatly influenced by the way they think. When people have irrational beliefs about themselves or the world, problems arise.

Because of this, the goal of the REBT is to help people change negative beliefs and patterns of thinking in order to overcome psychological problems and depression. REBT is organized and effective and has its own approach to counteracting and correcting distorted perceptions. Convincing and teaching, as well as collecting evidence, are important therapists' strategies for rational behavior.

Psychiatric therapy was created by Aaron Beck to provide systematic treatment for depression. Behavioral therapy is based on a hypothetical model: how we perceive situations influences how we feel emotionally. It helps clients identify their depressing thoughts and check how realistic the ideas are. Clients then learn to change their distorted thinking. When clients really think, they feel better. Emphasis also consistently on problem solving and initiating behavioral change.

Cognitive-behavioral modification (CBM) is a mental-behavioral therapy approach that focuses on transforming your negative speech and health accounts into positive self-expression. The basis of this treatment is that negative speech can manifest itself in a person's behavior. The goal of CBM is to change a person's story or life story from bad to worse. This is done by focusing on the strength and resilience of the client. CBM also helps clients forgive themselves for wrongdoing in the past and move forward with hope and hope for the future. With a positive change in the view and account of life, the client's actions and behavior will also change as expected.

XI
RUDIMENTARY IDEAS

CONTINUING ADVICE AND THEIR DIFFERENCES

Guidance refers to the advice and instructions given by a person who is knowledgeable or who has authority over various problems. Guidance occurs in almost every field; however, it is in the field of education that guidance is most often. Teachers, teachers, or professionals guide students on their educational paths. Counseling refers to the professional assistance provided by a counselor based on personal or psychological problems. In short, counseling is a form of personal guidance.

Therefore, unlike the usual guidance one can receive, counseling is usually intended to help people deal with minor psychological problems such as anxiety, depression, etc. Similarly, in order to be a qualified counselor, one must have extensive knowledge of education and training in the field of psychology and psychotherapy. the natural tendency to help people. The counselor works directly with the person in need of psychological help to alleviate his or her condition while guidance is available worldwide. The main objectives of the guide are to help each person understand and accept the positive and negative aspects of his or her personality, interests, fitness, attitude, etc. Provide a wide range of choices and opportunities and help shape a new lifestyle. This is a big difference between guidance and counsel.

ADVICE METHODS

In order to provide a framework for understanding how to apply counseling skills and strategies, we must first review the major legal theories that form the basis of different approaches.

THE PERSON'S WAY OF GETTING

A personal or client-focused approach was developed by Carl Rogers in the 1930s and 1940s. This theory is —your ‖ theory, based on the belief that people act according to how they think about themselves and their self-esteem is greatly influenced by their knowledge and others. It assumes that all people are intelligent, fair and able to take responsibility and make decisions that lead to independence, self-realization and independence. Moreover, this view is not concerned with moral causes or behavioral changes; rather, it focuses on the individual's current experiences, feelings, and actions.
The following are the major customer-focused structures:

1. Self-esteem encompasses personal opinion based on interaction with others.
2. A wonderful field is a real person and contains his own ideas and ideas about his world.
3. People will behave in a way that will enhance their self-esteem
4. Problems arise because of the conflict between self-esteem and personal experiences that lead one to use defenses such as denial or distortion of experiences that lead to pain and disorder.
5. It is only by receiving unconditional respect (acceptance) from other important people that people can be open and develop a more consistent relationship between self-esteem and behavior.

The goal of this treatment is to practice it and to see for yourself what can be achieved if there is a sympathetic relationship between the client and the counselor. Major wording techniques used by small counselors such as —Mm-hmm‖, —I see‖, and —yes‖. Counselor also uses reflection, clarification, summary and client approach.

The great advantage of this form of treatment is that this treatment provides a platform for individual recovery and growth. This approach meets all client needs at all levels, thus addressing all client-related issues that will lead to success. It also helps clients identify different paths

communication and thinking by expressing their feelings. The downside is that this treatment is highly hopeful and completely unregulated. In addition, it leaves the process to the client without considering the client seeking first aid which may lead to failure.

GESTALTAPPROACH

Gestalt therapy is experience (emphasizing doing and doing something, not just talking), presence (helps people make independent decisions and be responsible), and testing (encourages experimentation with new emotional expressions). _Gestalt 'is a German word meaning —statement‖. It was founded by Fritz Perls in the 1940's. All human behavior and experience are organized into Gestalt, where everything is larger than the sum of its parts. Individuals and their behavior should be considered complete. The body is contained within his nature through the boundaries of the ego. Nature is the source of jobs, people and knowledge to meet human needs. A self-aware person takes on the responsibility of searching in a place so that he can feed himself and be mentally stable.

The Gestalt approach is focused here and now. Only the 'way' and 'what' present 'are being asked and not' why 'and' when ', past or future. Emotions are considered a force. One has to develop self-awareness, acceptance, perfection and commitment to achieve a 'living balance'.

The main structures of Gestalt theory are:

1. (Full) maturity is achieved when people are able to combine their resources instead of using others and when they feed themselves instead of supporting the environment.

2. Awareness reduces avoidance behaviors that allow a person to deal with previously rejected and complete components.

3. Change occurs when people take responsibility and end an unfinished business (suppressed feelings related to past events that disrupt current operations)

4. The focus of treatment is on one's current feelings, thoughts, dreams, feelings, etc. and to encourage him to take ownership of these items in order to gain consolidation.

5. One is encouraged to rely on one's own understanding rather than on one's social status.

Gestalt therapy uses rules and games to increase customer awareness. Assistants ask clients to simulate conflict using simulation, exaggeration and reversal techniques and prevent the client from escaping the past or daydreaming about the future.

The great advantage of this method is that it is here and now and encourages clients to create more comfortable situations. The downside is that this approach focuses less on empathy and warmth and more on verbal and non-verbal behavior. In addition, it is contradictory and only works if the client believes in the effectiveness of the counselor as a physician.

PSYCHOANALYTICAPPROACH

Psychoanalytic therapy is a speech therapy based on the ideas of Sigmund Freud. This approach examines how the unconscious mind influences thoughts and behaviors, with the aim of providing insight and solutions to the person seeking treatment. Psychoanalytic therapy usually looks at a client's childhood experiences, to see if there are any events that have had a particular impact on their lives, or have somehow contributed to the current anxiety. This type of treatment is considered a long-term decision, and the duration may last for weeks, months, or even years, depending on the severity of the problem.

Psychoanalytic therapy is driven by understanding, so it looks to promote change by helping to understand a person's past and how events from a young person's life can affect a person now. The therapist will listen to the client's concerns and look for specific patterns or events that may be important. As well as listening to the client talk about his or her experiences and concerns, the therapist may use other techniques to help him or her identify and identify potential causes of anxiety, such as free association, treatment transfers and translation. Psychoanalytic function is best suited for common anxiety such as anxiety, relationship difficulties, sexual issues, low self-esteem, phobias, social embarrassment and difficulty sleeping.

Psychologists like Carl Jung believed in spiritual advancement and focused on combining conscious and conscious personality traits. Alfred Adler used techniques such as _psycho-education 'to promote public interest and to change erroneous thinking. On the other hand, ego psychologists and self-psychologists believed in the importance of the ego in relation to human development.

The great advantage of this method is that these methods are long-term which often produce better results and are based primarily on qondcognition‖. The biggest hurdle is that this approach is based on Freud's view of green and sexism. Moreover, they tend to overlook individual differences.

HOW TO EXPLAIN

Psychotherapy focuses on the belief that our thoughts are influenced by how we feel. There are a number of different treatments including Cognitive-Behavioral therapy, Reality therapy, and Rational Emotive therapy.

Mental-behavioral therapy focuses on systematic errors in thinking that cause psychological problems. It is given to Beck and uses techniques such as mental repetition, asking questions, searching for alternatives, monitoring thoughts, actual assessment, substitution, and teaching coping skills. True therapy is a treatment that focuses on problem solving and making better decisions to achieve specific goals. The point of this treatment is to help people make responsible decisions (including consistency between value systems and behavior) and to meet basic psychological needs without compromising the needs of others. Rational Emotive therapy (REBT) focuses on the belief that people have a tendency to develop behaviors and irrational beliefs. REBT acknowledges that past and present situations affect a person's thinking and uses a framework to enable the counselor to use open-ended events that allow the client to identify beliefs and outcomes. Finally, the Practical analysis is based on the idea that our personality consists of three levels of self-esteem - a parent, an adult and a child. Certain types of behaviors are associated with each role of the ego, and using this type of mentoring approach allows the client to understand the different stages of the ego and how it interacts with each other.

Psychotherapy focuses on the present. This means that stories of the past that influence current thinking are accepted but not focused on. Instead the counselor will work with the client to identify what is causing the distress in the current thinking. Self-confidence, role-playing and homework are also part of the individual support session the client will have with the counselor.

The great disadvantage is that its systematic nature may not be suitable for people with complex mental health or learning needs. difficulty.

TRAIT FACTORAPPROACH

Counseling techniques assume that job selection can be simplified and job outcomes are developed through a straightforward process of matching the most relevant aspects of a person's work (skills, interests, values, etc.) with information about job responsibilities, requirements, rewards, and availability. The counseling process for this approach usually begins with a client interview, then progresses to a broad psychological psychological evaluation of the factors associated with the client's work, and concludes with a description of the test results and links between these outcomes and one or more tasks. separation systems. Trait-Factor Counseling assumes that since they have been given accurate information about themselves and the tasks, most people will be able to choose a sensible career.

The main advantage of this method is that it laid the foundation for career counseling, is high in efficiency, and can be used by many people. Obstacles that exist are very direct and commanding. Moreover, it works by assuming that people will always make bad decisions that are not true.

BEHAVIOR AND ECECTIC

In terms of morality, human behavior is determined by its immediate effects on the environment (strengthening). Therefore, what is learned cannot be learned and human beings are considered to be viable living things. This view assumes that humans are incapable of controlling their behavior and that all behaviors are determined by natural selection.

Behavioral help is specifically targeted and controlled. The facilitator identifies bonds of incentive response (causes and effects of targeted behavior) and plans to disrupt or cancel these inappropriate bonds. The facilitator then puts them in a position to teach new bonds, which are more desirable for the renewal response as proper behavior will be learned. The four most common ways to change behavior are - (1) role-playing (modeling, teaching new behaviors through video or audio tape; (3) emotional therapy, _professional therapy '(a type of exposure treatment similar to imaginary flood techniques, in which anxiety is aroused to consider only the cause without direct communication), systematic sedation (aimed at eliminating the fear response of phobia, and instead of a relaxing response to conditional stimulus gradually using counter conditioning) and subtle sensitivity (unwanted behavior paired with an unpleasant image to eliminate that behavior); (4) a functional state, in which said to strengthen immediately using reinforcement schedules.

This approach is beneficial as it focuses on this and now instead of an intangible experience as seen in a psychodynamic / psychoanalytic approach. What's worse is the words that I can spell I often mistype. It relies too much on external factors —design‖ behavior.

An eclectic approach on the other hand is a treatment that combines a variety of therapeutic principles and philosophies to create the right treatment plan to meet the specific needs of a patient or client. The main advantage of eclectic therapy is that the treatment is customized to meet the unique needs of the patient. By creating a personalized medical experience to better address and respond to the needs of the patient, the eclectic therapist ensures that the most effective treatment strategies are integrated into the treatment. Any condition that can be treated with any type of treatment can be treated with eclectic therapy. Therefore, people with addiction, drug addiction, eating disorders, behavioral compulsions, emotional disorders, and other types of emotional or psychological problems can be successfully treated by a therapist who embraces eclectic therapy philosophy.

SHOWING WAYS

Assessment methods include many informal and informal tools and techniques, such as standard and informal assessments, questionnaires, inventory, checklists, observations, portfolios, performance appraisal, measurement scales, interviews, interviews, and more.

IMPORTANT THINGS

Some of the important things to consider when using testing are the following

· **Qualification**-Level testing evaluates what it should measure.

• **Reliability** - The degree to which an outcome of a measure, calculation, or specificity can depend on your accuracy.

• **Preparation** - Test / testing materials should not be biased.

• **Purpose** - The objective test has a positive and negative response that will be assessed in the same way for everyone who is being tested.

• **Scorability**- Refers to how easy it is to check to get points and the guidelines provided to get points.

• **Adequacy** - Tests should consist of a large range of material samples to determine outcomes or skills so that the outputs represent the population.

• **Management** - Assessment should be done uniformly for all learners so that the points obtained do not differ due to other factors.

• **Efficiency and efficiency** - Means the economy of time, effort and money in the test.

• **Code of Conduct** - Refers to maintaining confidentiality, distinguishing between right / wrong actions and following them properly.

• Counselors should also be responsible for proper use, score, interpretation, and use of appropriate assessment tools for the client.

• Counselors should carefully consider the suitability, reliability, psychometric limitations, and appropriateness of the tools when choosing a test.

• Counselors should conduct an assessment under the same circumstances established in their appointment.

• In the report of the test results, counselors must indicate the available bookings about legitimacy or reliability due to the testing conditions or the inadequacies of the test person.

TESTING TOOLS

• **Success tests** - Measure a person's level of knowledge in a particular area. They focus on individual knowledge as well as prior learning. Selected purposes are also used in educational institutions and the workplace. Example: TOEFL

• **Qualification assessment** - Qualification measures an individual's basic ability to acquire skills. This test has the potential to generate new information and is used to predict future performance. Common use of fitness assessments to predict client future performance in an educational program or job setting. Example: GATB

Desire and job evaluation-Desire is a person's willingness to do one or more specific tasks for others. These tests are used to measure and evaluate a person's level of interest, or choice, for different careers. Job Exams are processes used to assess a person's strengths, weaknesses, values and personality traits for different tasks. A counselor sometimes needs to help his clients make the difference between their interests and career realities. The idea is that if the client's interests are in line with the interests of the people in the intended project, he or she may be the right person for the intended job. Example: SCII, OSI, Ottis Employment Test

· **Personality testing** - Personality means permanent features that are different for each individual. These tests examine these factors and predict how each individual will react in the future in a particular situation. They also include reporting inventories and speculative audits. Example: MMPI, TAT, Rorschach inkblot test.

· **Intelligence Assessment** - Intelligence refers to the ability to acquire and apply information, to adapt to the environment, to learn experiences and to engage in a variety of thought processes. These tests are broad measurements of cognitive functioning. It can be an individual or a controlled group. They are used in educational institutions or to make assessment decisions. Example: WISC, Raven's Progressive Matrices.

In this Chapter, you will be introduced to the meanings of guidance and counsel and to the difference between the two. This unit also developed the basic methods of counseling and the pros and cons of each method. The key issues to consider in the assessment and the general framework of the various assessment tools have been discussed.

XII

SLAB IV: (COUNSELLING TECHNIQUES) GOALS OF COUNSELLING

People are looking for professional helpers where their capacity to meet complex health needs, where the growth they are seeking seems unattainable, where important decisions are elusive, and when environmental support systems are not available or inadequate. The purpose of counseling is to empower the client to cope with health conditions, reduce emotional stress, engage in productive work, and make effective decisions. As a result of counseling, counselors increase their control over current and future difficulties.

COUNSELLING PROCESS

The counseling process is a formal, formal conversation between the counselor and the client. It is a collaborative process in which a trained professional helps the client to identify the sources of difficulty they are facing. Together they formulate ways to deal with and overcome these problems so that the person grows to understand himself and others.

There are 5 stages in the counseling program-

1. Building relationships-

The first step involves building relationships and focusing on involving clients to explore issues that directly affect them. The initial dialogue is important as the counselor's verbal and non-verbal behavior greatly affects the client. The buyer will check two items-

(a) Compassion- The Counselor should go into the insscape 'of the client or be able to accurately hear the feelings and personal explanations the client is experiencing and speak to and accept the client.

(b) Integrity- The mentor should show compatibility between thoughts and feelings, should be spontaneous and show good consideration.

This is important in order to continue and make progress.

The following are some steps to build a relationship with a client-

- Introduce yourself
- Invite the client to sit down
- Make sure the client is comfortable
    - Invite a public discussion to reduce anxiety
    - View non-verbal behaviors as symptoms of a client's emotional state
- Show interest in the person
- Allow the client time to respond

2. Problem analysis-

While the mentor and client are in the process of establishing a relationship, a second process takes place. This is called problem detection. This step includes the collection and classification of information about the client's health status and the reasons for seeking counseling. This assessment can help the counselor obtain information about the client's current lifestyle, family history and personal history. This information can be used to plan appropriate counseling strategies and strategies.

3. Setting a goal-

As with any other activity, counseling should be focused. Terms refer to the outcomes or outcomes the client seeks to achieve at the end of counseling. The guidelines provide guidance on the counseling process. Terms should be carefully selected and defined.

The following are some guidelines for setting appropriate goals-

- The policies should relate to the client's desired outcome
- It has to happen
- Must be clear and measurable terms
- It should be said with encouraging words that emphasize growth

4. Counseling interventions-

There are different opinions about intervention depending on the theoretical view the counselor is subscribing to. For example, a person-centered approach suggests that the counselor should be involved rather than an intervention in the system; behavior is focused on activities to change or change client behavior.

5. Examination, termination or transfer-

All counseling is intended to end successfully. The elimination process should be done with extra sensitivity and care. Preparation for termination should begin long before it actually happens. It is also important to note that termination is not only necessary in the end, it is also possible when counseling seems unhelpful to the client. In this case, referring the client to another counselor may also work.

CHARACTERISTICS OF COUNSELLOR

The following are some of the characteristics of a counsellor-

- **Self-awareness-** Counsellors should be able to separate their needs,perceptions, and feelings from those of their clients and should be able to help others develop their own self-awareness.

- **Gender and cultural awareness**- Helpers who are sensitive to theinfluence of gender and culture on their own perceptions, values an attitudes are more likely to be open to the effects of these variables on others. Culturally sensitive helpers are likely to understand and feel comfortable with these differences and tend to value rather than denigrate these differences.
- **Honesty**- Honesty is more than just being truthful, it is also being opento exploration and being fair in evaluation. Helpers can communicate honesty by being open with clients, answering questions within professional limits, and by admitting mistakes or lack of knowledge. The helper must also invite honest feedback from clients and peers.
- **Congruence**- People have clarified and —own‖ their value systems arebetter able to these values and beliefs without imposing them on others, thus allowing a more honest and non-judgmental relationship.
- **Ability to communicate**- Developing and using communication skillscan have a positive effect on helping relationships.
- **Knowledge**- Professional helpers need knowledge of psychological,sociological and anthropological theory in order to help their clients effectively. However, experience is also necessary to increase helper adaptability.
- **Ethical integrity**- Ethical dilemmas are complex and challenging andmay arise regarding confidentiality, records, and type and length of service. Helpers need the capacity to tolerate ambiguity, uncertainty and ambivalence. They must know to put the client‘s welfare over their own needs or those outside of the organization.

GROUP COUNSELLING

Group counseling is a form of counseling in which a small group of people meet regularly to discuss, communicate, and assess problems with each other and with the group leader. Members gain insight into their thoughts and behaviors, and provide suggestions and support for others. In addition, people who have a difficult time in interpersonal relationships can benefit from social interaction which is a fundamental part of the group counseling experience. Most groups are made up of people of different ages, backgrounds, and experiences. This helps to provide additional ideas.

Group counseling helps to achieve the following goals-

? Provide and receive support
? Gain insight into problems and explore possible solutions
? Practice interpersonal skills in a safe group setting
? Learn more about how you interact with others
? Develop visual and feedback skills
? Develop problem-solving skills
? Improve expression
? Reduce social isolation
? Develop good communication skills

SPECIAL AREAS OF COUNSELLING

There are many special areas when counselling is considered. Here we will discuss about a few-

- **Vocational counselling-**Itis otherwise called as career counselling. Ithelps individuals and groups with career, personal goals, social and educational counselling. Many times, counsellors in this field work with individuals who feel unsatisfied with their career choices, but who are afraid to make changes because of emotional issues or family or financial constraints. This type of counsellor can work with people of all ages, from adolescents who want to explore career options to professionals who want to make career changes. Career counsellors typically have a background in vocational, industrial, or organizational psychology.
- **School counselling**- These counsellors help students at all levels tounderstand and cope with social, behavioral, and personal problems. School or education counsellors emphasize preventive and developmental counselling to enhance students' personal, social, and academic growth and to provide students with the life skills needed to deal with problems before they worsen. School counsellors often provide special services, including alcohol and drug prevention programs, conflict resolution classes, vocational counselling, and also try to identify cases of domestic abuse and other family problems that can

affect a student's development. School counsellors help students evaluate their abilities, interests, talents, and personalities to develop realistic academic and career goals.

- **Grief counselling**- These helpers practice a form of psychotherapy thataims to help people cope with grief and mourning following the death of loved ones, or with major life changes that trigger feelings of grief, such as divorce. There is a distinction between grief counselling and grief therapy. Counselling involves helping people move through uncomplicated, or normal, grief to health and resolution. Grief therapy involves the use of clinical tools for traumatic or complicated grief reactions. This could occur where the grief reaction is prolonged or manifests itself through some bodily or behavioral symptom, or by a grief response outside the range of a culturally-defined normality.
- **Financial counselling**-also is known as debt counselling, creditcounselling, or financial advising, depending upon the type of financial requirements that a person or family needs. While some counselling may deal with financial troubles, other forms of advisement can point to investments, asset allocation, and portfolio diversification. Counsellors in this field should have some training in investments, banking, and budgets.
- **Genetic counselling**- Genetic counselling is the process of advisingindividuals and families affected by or at risk of genetic disorders to help them understand and adapt to the medical, psychological and familial implications of genetic contributions to disease. These counsellors not only advise what to do but also provide support through the process, evaluate genetic test results, and also provide information on inheritance patterns in the family.
- **Rehabilitation counselling**- These counsellorsprovidecounselling,guidance and case management services to persons with disabilities to assist them in achieving their psychological, personal, social, and vocational goals. After conferring with the client's physicians, psychologists, occupational therapists, and the employer, a rehabilitation program is initiated. Rehabilitation counsellors are trained to recognize and to help lessen environmental and attitudinal barriers. Such help may include providing education, and advocacy services to individuals, families, employers, and others in the community. Rehabilitation counsellors work toward increasing the person's capacity to live independently by facilitating and coordinating

with other service providers.

- **Marital counselling**- These counsellors apply family systems theory,principles, and techniques to address and treat mental and emotional disorders. In doing so, they modify people's perceptions and behaviors, enhance communication and understanding among family members, and help to prevent family and individual crises. They may work with individuals, families, couples, and groups. Marriage and family therapy differs from traditional therapy because less emphasis is placed on an identified client or internal psychological conflict. The focus is on viewing and understanding their clients' symptoms and interactions within their existing environment

APPLIED AREAS IN MULTICULTURAL COUNSELLING

Multicultural counseling is the ability of any qualified counselor to receive counseling in the context of the client's country. In short, the cultural norms of the adviser or bias should not come first to the client. Ability in multicultural counseling is important in societies with multiple cultural groups whose social power and status qualifications are categorized based on physical (eg, race, gender) and intangible (e.g., homosexual / bizarre / transgender, language) attributes.

Multicultural counseling is concerned with the development of psychological functioning and the psychological and social (mal) improvement of clients given the disadvantaged social status due to membership of cultural groups. Regardless of their numerical representation in a particular society, these cultural groups are considered to be under the influence of social politics. As a result, they experience discrimination, prejudice, or oppression. These clients often leave early counseling sessions. To address this problem, the therapist's ability to earn credibility has been given great importance in order to achieve the best therapeutic effect. In other words, therapists and psychiatrists lose credibility when young clients lack the trust and confidence that their counseling concerns will be addressed in their cultural belief system. The credibility gained is related to the therapist's ability to provide interventions that are relevant to the client's belief system, as well as to provide appropriate and acceptable strategies to the client's cultural system.

Apart from honesty, social justice is the main concern of therapists and psychotherapy work that empowers and empowers young clients. Multicultural counseling, therefore, focuses on therapists' knowledge of complex factors that facilitate and hinder counseling relationships and strengths between therapists and clients from different cultural groups. It seeks to help clients with counseling concerns based on their low status to re-claim that the sources of stress are caused by circumstances rather than personal circumstances. In training and supervision, multicultural counseling analyzes whether power disparities due to counselor and group-client situations adversely affect the quality of therapeutic relationships, such as premature termination or allowing small and large clients. In addition to individual psychotherapy, multicultural counseling supports, as well as empowers, small clients to achieve social justice.

Overall, multicultural counseling incorporates therapist skills in the following three areas: (1) sensitive information on the impact of social pressure on identity development and client disputes,) and the ability to identify and apply cultural knowledge to instill trust and loyalty in a variety of medical relationships.

ETHICAL ISSUES

Some of the most important moral issues in our day are:

(1) Special communication and sharing of confidential information- In some cases, a counselor may be called to testify in a court of law in which the client's information may not be disclosed. This is called right communication. When confidentiality is considered, counselors can ask clients to sign an informed consent form and discuss openly what diagnostic criteria will be used. Counselors are also responsible for ensuring that their employer's union policies comply with their employment and personal codes.

(2) Conflicts of interest- It is important for counselors to remember that their primary function is during the process of assisting the client, not for another person or group. Therefore, in the event of a conflict of interest, counselors should ensure that they do not violate the client's privacy because of their ignorance, insecurity or incompetence, or for the benefit of a particular organization or group. The only reason for the violation of privacy is that the welfare of the client or another person is in danger.

(3) Record keeping - The Counselor must record only the purpose, the moral information and disclose the relevant material / explanations. If the counselor decides to use any other form of record keeping (cassette, computer archive, etc.), the client should be fully aware of what is going on.

(4) Use of computerized tests and programs - Advisers should only conduct tests if they have received adequate training and guidance in the administration of certain tests. They should also explain the reason and purpose of the test to the client. The big problem is the use of test data - who receives this data and what it will be used for. Without the clear oral consent of the client the matter should not be discussed with anyone.

(5) Dual relations- Dual relationships occur when a client assumes two different roles with a client. For example, one as a mentor the other as a sexual partner. Such relationships have a high potential for client abuse, which is less effective than counselor regardless of circumstances. Setting clear boundaries can be very helpful.

(6) Misrepresentation- Misrepresentation may occur when a counselor directly or indirectly imposes information, training, experience and or expertise on a particular client type or problem. They can work in such cases under surveillance / consultation with external specialists, refer to a specialist, or use joint therapy with a specialist.

(7) Multitasking- Failure to consider other diagnostic and therapeutic approaches, such as physical examination, psychopharmacology, or testing is another behavioral issue. For example, many clients experience stress that appears to be related to lower health conditions. A multi-faceted approach is needed such as mental and social flexibility
integrated symbols.

In this chapter, you have been informed of the counseling process and features of the counselor. The unit also highlighted the use of specialized counseling principles as well as a variety of ethical issues that counselors may face and how to deal with them.

XIII
COGNITIVE BEHAVIOUR MODIFICATION

Cognitive-behavioral modification (CBM) is a mental-behavioral therapy technique that focuses on transforming your negative speech and health accounts into positive self-expression. The basis of this treatment is that self-abuse can manifest itself in a person's behavior. The goal of CBM is to transform a person's story or life story from bad to worse. This is done by focusing on the strength and resilience of the client. CBM also helps clients forgive themselves for wrongdoing in the past and move forward with hope and hope for the future. With a positive change in perspective and life narrative, the actions and behaviors of the client will follow the same. CBM is a form of self-study therapy, which means that clients can do a lot of work and learn for themselves in their own time. In order for change, clients need to adjust their written behavior in order to be able to assess their behavior in a variety of contexts.

COGNITIVE RESTRUCTURING

Psychiatric reorganization, also known as cognitive reframing, is an approach to psychotherapy that can help people identify, challenge and change stress-related patterns and beliefs. The ultimate goal of psychological rehabilitation is to enable people to replace stress-induced thoughts with more precise and less complex thinking (and thus reduce stress). -or-anything (separation), magical thinking, repetition, magnification, and emotional thinking, often associated with many mental disorders. CR uses many techniques, such as Socrates questioning, recording thought, and target image, and is used in many forms of therapy, including psychotherapy. CBT) and treatment of rational emotive behavior (REBT).

Psychological rehabilitation refers to the process of behavioral psychotherapy to identify and replace negative and negative thoughts that contribute to the development of depression. This is done in collaboration between the client and the therapist, usually in the form of a conversation. For example, a college student may have failed math questions and replied, "That proves I'm stupid." The therapist may ask if that is what the test really means. To help the student determine the accuracy of the answer, the therapist may ask what grade the student has in math. If the student answers, "It's B," the therapist can then point out that his or her response shows that he or she is not stupid because he or she would not be stupid and get a B. Then together they can explore ways to rearrange what performance in question actually says. The answer to "I'm stupid" is an example of automatic thought. Depressed clients may have spontaneous thoughts in response to certain situations. They are automatic because they are spontaneous, negative, and do not come from intentional or logical thinking. This is often supported by negative or inaccurate thinking that dictates how patients view themselves, the situation, or the world around them.

The reorganization of the mind teaches us to stop relying on our automatic tendency to accept the content of our thoughts as an accurate examination of the truth. Rather, the goal is to begin by examining each step we take. It is an extremely powerful treatment modified to help people deal with all kinds of stressful situations and situations. Another setback is that it is difficult for people to learn about self-help (without the help of a therapist). It is easy for people to assume that they are doing it right when they are not and to falsely assume that this process is ineffective.

1 Role of Cognitive Restructuring in Cognitive Behavioral Therapy

Cognitive Behavioral Therapy, or CBT, is based on the idea that the way we think affects the way we feel. It is easy to see the concept behind this view, as well as the effects of erroneous thinking. Psychological reorganization was first introduced as a therapeutic tool for CBT and Rational Emotive Behavioral Therapy, or REBT. CBT physicians quickly discovered that it was a flexible and flexible tool that could help many people dealing with all kinds of problems, whether the problems were caused by external factors, internal problems, or both. This approach to stress management and promoting healing makes for a multitude of CBT sessions and offers a wide range of techniques and exercises that can be applied to almost any client situation. Used properly, it can help a client learn to stop relying on his or her own ideas as a true advocate and begin to evaluate his or her thoughts more accurately.

2 Key Components of Cognitive Restructuring

In order to achieve system change, the effective mind-altering system (CR) has three key components. Each of these components is essential for success. If any component is missing, the intervention will not include CR but another type of intervention. Each component may have different intervention strategies, but combined empiricism interactions, verbal interventions, and hypothesis-empirical tests form the treatment process involved in CR. The following gives a description and illustration of these three central CR features.

Collaborative empiricism.Beck and colleagues introduced the term "co-empiricism" to describe the therapeutic relationships found in CR. The concept has been refined and interpreted by subsequent clinical researchers and is now considered an important component of CT or CBT practice. In essence, empiricism collaboration involves the client and the therapist sharing their expertise to explain, explain, and help solve client problems. Recognizing their contributions to the medical profession, the therapist as a specialist in the transformation process, and the client as a living experience of the problem, work together to formulate treatment goals, set a session agenda, and discuss homework. The therapist and the client share an equal responsibility for treatment guidance, with the therapist often seeking feedback and ensuring client understanding.

A strong medical alliance and client involvement in the treatment process is a necessary but insufficient aspect of effective CR. In order to achieve a collaborative environment, the therapist (a) teaches the client a CT model to establish a consistent reason for achieving change, (b) involves the client in identifying and prioritizing treatment goals, (c) works together to set a session agenda,

(d) ask questions and request customer feedback at all times, and (e) discuss household chores. This strong emphasis on uniform responsibility and participatory participation in the treatment process ensures that CR does not become a dictator, with the therapist placing ideas and guidance on the client. An authoritative, extremely confusing, and uncompromising style will quickly undermine the effectiveness of CR.

Empiricism is another central aspect of the treatment process in CR. The therapist encourages the client to take a research approach, asking questions about long-held beliefs and attitudes. Throughout the treatment, emphasis is placed on observation, experience testing, and learning. The therapist uses Democratic questions about previous personal knowledge to assess the validity of erroneous beliefs and to offer a chance for a different perspective. In addition, experience-based tests are created that can legally validate the validity of another belief and challenge the validity of the wrong schemes. The psychiatrist often encourages the client to "check this with your knowledge, ‖ or — gather some evidence and see what can be learned. Effective participatory empiricism will more easily encourage clients to incorporate behavioral change into their efforts instead of external power or therapist skills. This self-determining trait should result in better and more lasting treatment outcomes.

Verbal interventions.

Over the years psychiatric researchers and physicians have developed a myriad of interventions that can be used directly by therapists to reverse maladaptive schematic content. These strategies, which are the main components of CR, are listed below. The first four strategies are the most commonly used oral interventions in CR, first introduced by Beck et al. in early CT medical literature and later refined and interpreted by other psychiatrists. Collecting evidence, analyzing costs / benefits, identifying cognitive errors, and producing other explanations is such an important part of CR that using these verbal interventions is what many therapists think of as psychological reorganization. They are healthy and practical steps that can be applied to many clinical problems.

Strategies for Interpreting Words in the Psychological Rehabilitation Program are listed below:

1. Evidence-gathering - Obtaining schema-related evidence from past and current client experiences that allows for more balanced evaluation of program content.

2. Consequential analysis - Evaluating the immediate and long-term costs and benefits of continued acceptance of a false belief.

3. Cognitive Bias Identification - Train clients to be more aware of active psychological bias when processing schema-related information (e.g., different thinking, disaster risk, psychological learning, magnification / reduction, etc.)

4. Generate Alternative - Creates a flexible concept of personal and / or specific aspects of personal information that more accurately represent external emergencies and that improve client adaptability.

5. Familiarity - Recognizing unwanted thoughts, feelings and behaviors such as deviations from normal human experience in order to promote greater acceptance and confidence in dealing with the schema-related experience.

6. Disaster devastation - Creating a predictable account of the worst case scenario, assessing its real and potential impact on quality of life and developing a disaster response strategy.

7. Problem Solving - Defining a real-life problem, explaining the pros and cons of various responses to a problem, choosing a course of action, and evaluating the outcome.

8. Figurative exposure - Directing the client to repetitive and systematic production of thought, image, or unnecessary schema-related emotions in order to improve client efficiency in dealing with unwelcome emotions.

9. Distance - Teaching clients to take a 'third party' or someone watching their unwanted thoughts and feelings; reactions to their thoughtful experiences as if they belonged to someone else.

10. Frame resizing or taking a view - Focusing on the current experience as a moment of time and stopping it for a longer lifetime

11. Rehabilitation - Identifying the external or environmental causes of a client's difficulties in order to deal with internal exaggeration and self-criticism.

12. Good Redirecting - Re-focusing the client on a positive, flexible experience that provides non-schema information.

In order to implement any of these oral interventions, clients must be willing to engage in the assessment process. That is, they should be willing to at least consider the possibility that their thinking of the wrong framework may be wrong, contradictory, and unreasonable. Clients who insist that their misconceptions are undeniable facts will not be open to CR. Second, the therapist always begins by inviting clients to explore and evaluate their thoughts and beliefs with strong evidence, that is, their personal knowledge. The therapist avoids getting upset, arguing, or trying to convince the client with another contextual belief instead of clinging to the idea of a wrong plan. Instead, clients are encouraged to create an alternative perspective that provides a better understanding of — purpose— and external experience and that can be associated with progress in their emotional functioning. Third, effective CR will ensure equal emphasis on questioning the validity of misconceptions and assessing the compatibility of different contextualisation. The purpose of CR is to raise doubts in the mind of the customer about long-held wrong beliefs (e.g., antuPeople will notice that I'm worried and think something is wrong with me‖) and consider the accuracy and functioning of a different opinion (e.g., antuPeople may see that I am a little worried but take it as insignificant‖).

3. Applications within therapy

There are many methods used in the reconstruction of the mind, which often involve identifying and writing distorted thoughts, such as "all or no thinking, good prevention, mental filtering, jumping to conclusions, catastrophic, emotional thinking, statements to be made, and human actions". The following methods are often used in mind reorganization:

Socrates questions

Socrates' questions are a type of straightforward questionnaire that can be used to pursue thought in many ways and purposes, including: exploring complex ideas, reaching facts, uncovering problems and problems, revealing ideas, analyzing ideas, analyzing what we can and cannot do, following logical results or controlling conversations. Democratic questions are based on the premise that thinking is rational, and allows lesser ideas to be answered. The key to distinguishing Socrates 'questions and questioning each other is whether Socrates' questions are organized, instructive, deep and often focus on basic concepts, principles, theories, issues or problems. Socrates' collection of questions in psychiatry aims to address the underlying thoughts that oppress a patient:

1. **Identifying the problem:** 'What evidence supports the theory? And what proof is there of it? '

2. **To consider some practical alternatives:** 'What could be another explanation or view of the situation? Why did it happen again? '

3. **Examine the various potential side effects:** 'What are the worst, the best, most tolerable and real effects?'

4. **Analyze the consequences:** 'What is the effect of thinking or believing this? What would be the result if you did not come to terms with your situation in a different way and thus lose your temper? '

5. **Distance:** 'Think of a friend / family member who is in a similar situation or if they were in a similar situation, what would I say to them?'

Careful use of Socrates' questions enables the therapist to challenge recurring or isolated situations of mindless thinking while maintaining an open space that respects inner thinking and even seemingly irrational thoughts.

Imagination of thought

Keeping a record of thoughts is a great way to help you or your client identify any undiagnosed or unrecognized distortions, which is the first step needed to rearrange them. There are several different ways to organize a thought text, but the main idea is to note what repetitive thoughts come to mind and the situations from which they come. Typically, a thought record instructs the client to record the mood, thoughts, feelings, behavior, and other thoughts.

Identifying cognitive errors

The person is also asked to begin identifying the types of mental disorders in which they share the color of their perception of circumstances. This may include the following:

· Decreased performance —If I can, it doesn't count‖

• All or nothing to think —I pass or fail‖, —We win or lose‖, ‖Or or wrong‖, ikwI do everything now or do nothing at all‖.

• Label —I did something wrong so I'm bad—, I said something stupid so I'm stupid‖

• Mind learning —He did not look at me so I did something wrong‖

• Divination —I just know it will be worse ‖

• Making disaster —Oh my God it is so bad‖

• Personalization —It's all my fault‖, —I'm to blame‖

• Blaming —is all his fault‖

• Normal — I don't get what I want‖, — always ‖

• I should, I should, I should have the tools and the things that iname / you / he / she should... should... should....

Destruction

This process basically asks —what is the worst possible? ‖ And following the situation to the end. People are often troubled by thoughts or concerns about the worst possible outcome, even if that effect (a) is very unlikely, and (b) will not ruin our lives even if it does!

Ending the crisis or wondering —what will happen? Will help you or your client decide what to do, reduce unreasonable or unreasonable concerns, and see that even the worst situations can be controlled.

Directed Images

Visualization can be a wonderful tool for relaxation, pain control, anxiety management, and anger control. It is also the most effective form of mental rehabilitation.

• Recognizing a Life Event - This process involves having the client identify a specific event or theme focused on treatment sessions.

• Dream Recovery or Day Photo - This photo process focuses on a specific image a client already has. An image can be what a client experienced in a dream, dream, dream or previous session of a targeted image. Wherever it comes from, it will capture the natural instinct of the consumer and may cause the client to feel anxious, sad, angry, or some other extreme emotion.

• Focused Feeling - The type of final image is characterized by the client focusing on the feeling they have in the session, and allowing the image to come out of the feeling. The image will usually appear automatically, but if not, a method called multisensory evocation can help clarify the image. In this way, the therapist will guide the client by examining the nerves to help sharpen the image and point out more details.

4 Criticisms

Critics of cognitive restructuring claim that the process of challenging dysfunctional thoughts will teach clients to become better suppressors and avoiders of their unwanted thoughts. And that cognitive restructuring shows less immediate improvement because real world practice is often required. Other criticisms include that the approach is mechanistic and impersonal and that the relationship between therapist and client is irrelevant.

MEICHENBAUM'S SELF STRUCTIONAL TRAINING

Donald Meichenbaum is a psychologist noted for his contributions to behavioral psychotherapy (CBT). He developed a treatment called cognitive behavior modification (CBM), which focuses on identifying ineffective self-expression in order to change unwanted behavior. Meichenbaum views behavior as the result of our own accountability. Self-education is an intellectual approach that aims to give clients control of their behavior through self-reported gradual hidden and self-created guidance. This is especially helpful when there is a lack of motivation at first for example to solve problems or to discuss words that contribute to difficulty. This approach suggests that behavior change can be done if clients are encouraged to change the instructions they give themselves, in the form of 'self-expression', into dynamic versions. These internal conversations are taken out during treatment and discussed, and strategies are developed to deal with them. These strategies include relaxation, small voice instructions (such as telling yourself to "stop!" Thoughts, called _ stop thinking '), and simulation programs.

Self-education is crucial in coping with stressful situations, and has led Meichenbaum to develop 'jo injection training'. In this process, people first ask how they feel about stressful situations — for example, they might say 'I can't handle the situation'. They are then encouraged to develop and familiarize themselves with positive statements such as' Anxiety will not help ',' one step at a time 'and' may be worse ', and reinforce self-expression

such as' that' was better '. As well as being used in the industry to manage stress, such procedures have been used to treat anxiety and speech disorders, phobias, schizophrenia, and overweight in children.
The most important role assigned to cognitive functions not only challenges the traditional doctrines of behavioral medicine but also enhances and enhances the very specific processes that have emerged in the field in recent years. Educational training, first used with dysfunctional children to change negative thinking processes, and stress inoculation training, used successfully both in the clinic and at high risk for people entering the clinic to help them change attitudes, use coping skills, and cope effectively with stressful situations, illustrate. opportunities for a broader approach.

Psychological reorganization plays an important role in Meichenbaum's (1977) approach. He describes the formation of the mind as part of the planning process of thought, which seems to monitor and direct the selection of thoughts. Meichenbaum's self-discipline training focuses on helping clients become more self-reliant. The treatment process involves teaching clients to make their own statements and training clients to change the instructions they give them so that they can deal with the problems they face. Together, the therapist and the client practice self-discipline and desirable behavior in role-playing situations that mimic stress situations in the daily life of the client. Emphasis on acquiring practical skills to deal with problematic situations such as impulsive behavior and aggression, fear of experimentation, and fear of public speaking.

5 Behavior Changes

Meichenbaum (1977) argues that koku behavioral change occurs in a series of mediation processes that include internal communication, thought structures, and behavior and its resulting consequences‖. Describes the process of three stages of change in which those three components are integrated. According to him, focusing on one aspect will probably not be enough.

Stage 1: Self-examination. The first step in the transformation process consists of clients learning to monitor their behavior. When clients start treatment, their internal dialogue is characterized by negative statements and pictures. An important factor is determination and the ability to listen. This process involves more sensitivity to their thoughts, feelings, actions, physical reactions, and ways of responding to others.

If depressed clients hope to make positive changes, for example, they should first realize that they are not —a victims of negative thoughts and feelings. Rather, they are actually contributing to the depression of the things they tell. Although self-examination is necessary in the event of a change, it is not enough for the change. As treatment progresses, clients discover new thinking structures that allow them to look at their problems in a new way. This rethinking process arises through a collaborative effort between the client and the therapist.

Step 2: Starting a new internal dialogue. As a result of contact with the first client of the client, clients learn to recognize their inappropriate behavior, and begin to see the potential for dynamic behaviors. If clients are hoping to change what they tell themselves, they should start a new series of behaviors, which are not in line with their inappropriate behavior. Clients are learning to change their internal conversation about treatment. Their new internal dialogue serves as a guide for new behaviors. Next, this process has an impact on customer perceptions.

Phase 3: Learning new skills. The third phase of the transformation process consists of teaching clients effective coping skills, which are practiced in real-life situations. (For example, clients who are unable to cope with failure may avoid attractive jobs for fear that they will not succeed. Psychological reorganization may help them change their negative thinking, thus making them more willing to participate in desirable activities.) At the same time. , clients continue to focus on inventing new sentences and looking at and evaluating results. Because they behave differently in situations, they often experience different reactions from others. The stability of what they learn is greatly influenced by what they themselves say about their newly acquired behavior and its consequences.

6 BECK'S MODEL

Aaron Beck is considered the father of psychiatry. Beck developed psychotherapy in the belief that human experience triggers perceptions or thoughts. This understanding is linked to schemes, which are fundamental beliefs formed from an early age, in order to shape our view of the world and to determine our emotional and moral state. Psychiatric treatment is based on an intellectual perspective of psychopathology. A mental model describes how people's perceptions, or spontaneous thoughts about situations, influence their emotional, behavioral (and often physical) reactions.

Individual opinions are often distorted and do not work out when they are stressed. They can learn to identify and evaluate "spontaneous thinking" (verbal comprehension or spontaneous imagination), and to adjust their thinking to be more accurate. When they do, their stress often subsides, they are able to behave more efficiently, and (especially anxiously) their dramatic physical awakening recognizes and transforms their distorted beliefs: their basic understanding, their worlds, and other people. These distorted beliefs influence their processing of information, and they cause their distorted thinking.

Therefore, the model of understanding describes people's emotional, physical, and behavioral responses as guided by their perceptions of experience, influenced by their beliefs and their fundamental ways of dealing with the world, and knowledge itself. Physicians use Socrates' gentle questioning technique to help clients evaluate and respond to their own automatic ideas and beliefs — and to teach them to participate in the testing process themselves. Therapists can also help clients design behavioral tests that will be performed between sessions to assess comprehension in a predictive manner. When client thoughts work, therapists resolve problems, evaluate patients' conclusions, and work with them to accept their difficulties.

An understanding model describes how people's thoughts and ideas influence their lives. Often, stress can distort people's judgment, and that can lead to negative emotions and behavior. CBT helps people learn to identify and evaluate their "automatic thoughts" and transform their thinking into healthy ones. The psychiatric model is central to CBT, and plays an important role in helping clinicians use Socrates' gentle questions to improve their treatment. The Cognitive Triad is a comprehensive model developed by Aaron Beck to explain the cause of depression. He suggested that three types of negative thoughts lead to depression: thoughts about yourself, the world / environment, and the future. People suffering from depression will say that bad and unpleasant experiences are the result of their own (personal) failure and of an unjust and unforgiving world. The future is considered miserable and hopeless for their lasting problems.

The components of the three feeds also reinforce negative ideas in one place making the other parts of the triangle stronger. Signs of events arise from mistaken beliefs about the individual, the world, and the future. Psychotherapy focuses on altering these negative attitudes to reduce bad symptoms. This can be done by reflecting on the good qualities of the depressed patient, the country, and its future.

7 ELLIS'S RATIONAL EMOTIVE THERAPY

Rational Emotive Therapy, sometimes called Rational Emotive Behavioral Therapy, is a form of behavioral psychology based on behavior. It tries to use common sense and common sense to detect isolated mental processes, and learns to express emotions more appropriately. Effectively, the theory is that careless harmful behavior is consciously acknowledged and replaced by positive behavior.Rational-Emotive-Behavior Therapy (REBT), developed by Albert Ellis, is a treatment that carefully uses cognitive, emotional, and behavioral strategies. to help clients. REBT experts emphasize that people have decisions. Control of thoughts, attitudes, feelings, and actions is direct for a person who plans to live according to personal instructions. With little control over what is happening or what is really going on, people are able to choose and control how they view the world and how they respond to adversity.

Rational-Emotive-Behavior Therapy (REBT) has emerged from what Albert Ellis considers to be a limited therapeutic approach to treatment that uses careful thinking, emotional, and behavioral techniques to help clients. Ellis sees himself as a philosopher or academic who uses a didactic, focused, and descriptive approach to change.

Based on the perception that what worries people is not the event but their judgment of the event, REBT experts emphasize that people are able to make informed choices. Control of thoughts, attitudes, feelings, and actions is direct for a person who plans to live according to personal instructions. With little or no control over what is happening or what is actually going on, humans have both the ability to choose and to control how they view the world and how they respond to adversity.

Ellis regarded people as naturally irrational, self-absorbed people who wanted to be taught to change crooked thinking by removing the virtues, the right, the proper, and the requirements to overcome them. People can be helpful and loving as long as they do not think rudely. The three areas in which people cling to irrational beliefs are based on the assumption that they must be perfect, that others must be perfect, and that the earth must be a perfect place to live. The goal of therapy is to teach people to think and behave in a way that satisfies the individual by making them realize that they have a choice between self-harm, bad behavior and thought as well as effective, progressive, and positive behavior. This is accomplished by teaching people to commit to their own logical thinking and consequences or behavior that follows.

Ellis developed the belief that the system of belief - what people tell themselves about an event - determines the answers or feelings about that event. People naturally and easily think of themselves as being crooked, expressing emotions in a negative way and behaving in a self-destructive way. REBT teaches you how to do something different. Unreasonable beliefs create problems. A list of common sense beliefs that lead to negative feelings and pressure on children, teens, and parents is included in the chapter.

Ignorant beliefs can create a series of additional irrational beliefs. The categories of those ideas are self-deprecating beliefs, strong and solid beliefs, anti-social beliefs, irrational beliefs and conflicting beliefs.

The goal of the REBT is to teach people to think and behave in a way that satisfies themselves by making them realize that they have a choice between self-harm, bad behavior and effective, positive, positive behavior. The primary purpose of therapy is to show a person how irrational beliefs or attitudes cause ineffective effects such as anger, depression, or anxiety. The second goal is to teach the client how to refute or break down irrational beliefs and replace them with rational ideas. This will allow the client to escape the cycle of negative emotions and be free to choose behavior that eliminates the problem or the negative impact of the problem.

"A, B, C, D, and E" refers to these ideas. A is an active event. B is how a person reacts to an event. C stands for results or feelings that are the result of one's exploring the event. D stands for controversial arguments that can be used to attack your personal nonsensical messages that are embedded in a snapshot event. E are the answers given to the questions raised in D. REBT is direct, confusing, direct and indirect counseling. There are a number of factors that help counselors get the most out of their thinking. They can look at the ordinary, the perversion, the removal, the catastrophe, the total, the criticism and fortune-telling. When irrational beliefs are identified, the counselor opposes them and challenges them. The ultimate goal is for young people to see their absurd beliefs, reflect on them, and reject them.

REBT counselors use assessment, ventilation, interpreting, coping, teaching and re-teaching. Counselors teach and often provide homework. With children counselors can find work in internal communication and role-changing techniques are helpful. Rational-emotive-behavioral education is a breed of REBT that focuses on how emotions develop, how to distinguish between right and wrong speculation, and how to think logically.

Behavioral therapy programs (CBT) are examples of integration and behavioral approaches. The practice of CBT incorporates behavioral change methods and thought testing methods to produce behavior and a sense of change in clients. Pressure injection methods combined with simulation provide an example of CBT. For the treatment of childhood depression, CBT has four levels of treatment: (1) behavioral processes, such as concomitant strengthening, formation, motivation, and modeling, increasing social interaction; (2) CBT interventions, which include matching the successful completion of work with positive statements and reinforcement of those statements; (3) psychological interventions, used for community skills training, role-playing, and self-regulation; and (4) self-control procedures, such as self-assessment and strengthening. CBT is used successfully in treating anger, anxiety, depression, ADHD, obesity, and children with alcoholism.

KEY CONCEPTS

1. Rational-emotive-behavioral therapy focuses on present events and the person's reaction to those events.

2. According to REBT, people have almost complete responsibility for their ideas and for their feelings.

3. The role of the counsellor is to attack the false beliefs that cause negative reactions to events.

4. Cognitive-Behavior therapy combines behavior-change methods with thought-restructuring methods to produce behavior and feeling change in clients.

5. Cognitive-behavior therapy involves cognitive restructuring, cognitive behavior modification, and stress inoculation.

6. It is better for people to focus on negating specific behaviors than to develop a negative self-image.

7. The "A, B, C, D, and E" approach shows how problems develop and how to treat them.

8. Effective strategies with children include direct teaching of concepts, such as teaching the child to like oneself, to not take things too seriously, to realize that there is joy in participation, to realize that achievement requires effort, or to realize that one does not have to be perfect.

KEY TERMS AND CONCEPTS

—A,B,C,D, and E‖ approach – The rational-emotive behavioral approach to counselling. The A, B, C shows how problems develop (A=activating event, B=how the event is evaluated, C=consequences), and the D, E are the treatment steps (D=disputing arguments, E=answers you have developed).

Circle of irrational thinking – A process of thinking that leads to self-hate, which leads to self-destructive behavior, which leads to hatred of others, and eventually causes individuals to act irrationally toward self, thus continuing the cycle.

Contradictory beliefs – An irrational belief that originates from false premises.

Dogmatic beliefs – An irrational belief that leads to unrealistic preferences and wishes.

Irrational beliefs – Statements that individuals tell themselves that create dysfunctional consequences such as anger, depression, or anxiety.

REBE – Rational Emotive Behavior Education. The objectives of REBE include teaching how feelings develop and how to think rationally

Self-defeating beliefs – An irrational belief that interferes with basic goals and drives.

Stress-inoculation – Cognitive techniques designed to help people master difficult and highly stressful situations and events that they anticipate that they will encounter in the future.

THOUGHT STOPPING AND VARIATIONS

The human brain is often full of questions and internal conversations. For the last few artists, our minds can simultaneously jump from happiness to trouble to politics to romance to the price of tea. For some people, negative or fearful thoughts can be normal and repetitive, leading to panic attacks, anxiety, fear, depression, or forced mental disturbances. Some psychologists try to help those who suffer from these disorders in a way that is known as hallucinations.

The basic concept of mindfulness revolves around finding ways to re-focus the mind away from what causes stress. For example, in the case of anxiety or panic, a person often realizes that his fears of something or situation are unreasonable. However, the more he thinks about not getting into a panic, the more likely he is to panic. These problems can be so severe that they can withdraw from any stressful situation, leading to even greater anxiety, depression, and social isolation. Often there are biological or genetic causes in such cases, and stopping thinking is a concept of understanding. a tool that is widely used in conjunction with medicine, medicine, or both. The goal is to help the sufferer to live a happy and successful life. Stopping thinking is not the perfect solution or solution, but it is one of the ways to win.

Stopping a thought involves focusing on a thought you do not want for a moment, then suddenly stopping and pouring out your mind. The internal command —Stop! ‖ Or cut off the rubber band on the wrist is often used to interrupt an unpleasant thought. One of the oldest forms of thinking that is still commonly used is that of cessation of the mind, introduced by Bain in 1928 in his book Thought Control in Everyday Life. In the late 1950's, Joseph Wolpe and other moral scientists were transformed into depressing and phobic minds. Mindfulness has been shown to be effective in many stressful and discriminatory thought processes: sexual preoccupation: hypochondriasis, depressive thoughts of failure, sexual dysfunction, depressing memories, and panic, recurring feelings that lead to chronic depression and anxiety attacks. While mindfulness is only effective in about 20 percent of cases involving forced behavior, it is more than 70 percent effective in controlling thoughts about simple phobias such as fear of snakes, driving, darkness, elevators, and someone hiding in the house. at night, fear of madness, and so on. Thought-setting is recommended when problem behavior is primarily psychological rather than practical. It is shown when certain thoughts or images are repeatedly found to be painful or lead to unpleasant emotional states.

PROBLEM SOLVING TECHNIQUES

Behavioral therapies are proven evidence-based methods of altering thoughts, feelings, and behavior and improving health and performance satisfaction. They are informed of the most recent psychological research, which has repeatedly shown that it is among the most effective interventions for emotional disorders and psychological problems. The behavioral therapies listed below represent some of the most common CBT procedures designed to improve mood and behavior.

Psychological Rehabilitation Methods: Psychiatric rehabilitation is a behavioral therapy approach aimed at helping people identify thought patterns that are responsible for negative emotions and dysfunctional behaviors. There are many techniques used during mental reorganization. The most common way is to track negative thoughts in the form of a thought record, and to establish healthy, thought-provoking thinking patterns.

Graduation Activities in Grades: Exposure is a behavioral therapy that helps people get closer to what they are afraid of. Often, fear causes people to avoid situations. Unfortunately, avoiding frightening situations is what keeps the feelings of fear and anxiety at bay. With formal exposure, people are well aware of the horrific situations one by one, and then face difficult exposure assignments. Exposure is one of the most effective psychiatric treatments available, with a 90% efficacy and some anxiety disorder.

Career Planning: Career planning is a comprehensive treatment designed to help people develop the behaviors they should be doing the most. By identifying and planning useful behaviors, such as meditation, hiking, or working on a project, you increase your chances of success. This method is especially useful for people who are not actively engaged in lucrative careers because of stress, or who are having difficulty completing tasks due to procrastination.

Sequential Evaluation: This method of psychotherapy works for people who have difficulty finishing a job, either because they do not know the job well, or because the job feels overwhelmed for some reason. This app works by helping people do a simple task like a very difficult task. It's like getting used to mixing and subtracting before learning to separate for a long time. Once you are trained to add and subtract, long-term separation is not so easy. Similarly, by repeating the same behavior, the more difficult ones feel controlled.

Practicing Contemplation: Contemplation is a psychological therapy borrowed from Buddhism. The goal of awareness is to help people avoid rushing or focusing on negative things and re-focusing their attention on what is really happening in the present. Meditation is the subject of a relatively new study in psychology and represents the edge of psychotherapy practice.

Skills Training: Many people's problems are caused by a lack of the right skills to achieve their goals. Skills training is a form of behavioral therapy used to address those skills shortages. Typical areas of skills training include community skills training, communication training, and strength training. Skills training usually takes place through direct teaching, modeling, and role-playing games.

Another great alternative to mindfulness therapy is Donald Meichenbaum's cognitive behavior modification (CBM), which focuses on changing the client's response. The basic premise of CBM is that clients, as a requirement for behavior change, should be aware of how they think, feel, and behave and the impact it has on others. In order for change, clients need to adjust their written behavior in order to be able to assess their behavior in a variety of contexts. Psychological reorganization plays an important role in Meichenbaum's (1977) approach. Psychological reorganization or reorganization of the mind refers to the process of behavioral psychotherapy to identify and replace negative and negative thoughts. It is a psychotherapeutic process of learning to identify and counteract irrational or negative thoughts known as mental distortions, such as all-or-nothing thinking (divisions), magical thinking, overproduction, nurturing, and emotional thinking, often associated with many mental health problems.CR uses many techniques, such as questioning. Democratic, imaging, and imagery, and is used in a wide variety of therapies, including behavioral psychotherapy (CBT) and rational emotive behavior therapy (REBT). Numerous studies show great effectiveness in using CR-based therapies.

Beck developed psychotherapy in the belief that human experience triggers perceptions or thoughts. This understanding is linked to schemes, which are fundamental beliefs formed from an early age, in order to shape our view of the world and to determine our emotional and moral state. Psychiatric treatment is based on an intellectual perspective of psychopathology. A mental model describes how people's perceptions, or spontaneous thoughts about situations, influence their emotional, behavioral (and often physical) reactions.

Rational Emotive Therapy, sometimes called Rational Emotive Behavioral Therapy, is a form of behavioral psychology based on behavior. It tries to use common sense and common sense to detect isolated mental processes, and learns to express emotions more appropriately. Effectively, the view is that harmful behavior can be overlooked and consciously accepted and dismissed as more constructive behavior. Rational-Emotive-Behavior Therapy (REBT), developed by Albert Ellis, carefully uses cognitive, emotional, and behavioral techniques to assist clients. REBT experts emphasize that people have decisions.

XIV

PROFESSIONAL PREPARATION & EXERCISE

Counseling involves working with different people and dealing with their daily problems in individual, family, or group settings. Counseling psychologists often work to help clients with a variety of problems, often minor complications. The psychologists who are counseled are often influenced by the theoretical direction in which they adhere. There are a number of theoretical positions, each providing a different meaning behind the causes of mental disorders and their appropriate treatment. The purpose of the counselor is to provide support to clients' goals by helping to reduce stress, by assisting in the effort to provide a healthy environment, to help them focus on personal goals and condoms, thus contributing to client motivation, performance, and satisfaction with their health. The counselor listens, understands, and directs better understanding among the people involved. A non-judgmental attitude and confidentiality agreement are part of the whole process.

Effective counselors are those who have a mature, balanced outlook on life, who can put themselves in the shoes of those who have a sense of humor and who are able to respect their ideas, thoughts, feelings, and emotions. There are many factors to consider when training for the role of mentor, and education professionals need to focus on training students to enter and thrive in this important field.

CHOICE

It is increasingly recognized in any professional field that entrants should be carefully selected. It is not enough to focus only on the features of intelligence or interest expressed in the service to the client. The personality traits of counselors are of great importance. The success of the mentor is said to depend on the goals that they are trying to achieve. The counselor must be sensitive to the circumstances and needs of the people and, above all, be honest and sincere.

The first and most important requirement for professional counselors is the necessary skills and knowledge. Professional training and skills should be regularly reviewed and updated. Training can be basic or general and / or the training of different professionals depending on the area or groups or circumstances in which they can work.

All fields of expertise consider the importance of selecting the right people to be trained to become members of a particular field. In order to set the right goals it is necessary to identify the different roles of counselors. Counseling is basically a job of helping. Therefore, it is closely related to the needs and characteristics of the social system in which it must function and function, as well as resources; labor and material; found in the system.

SKILLS

A balanced and dreamy mentoring training program should include the following to train prospective mentors with the relevant knowledge, skills and competencies needed for the job:

Basic theoretical correction: Understanding motivation, flexibility in human correction, learning principles and other concepts that support counseling, psychosocial principles and procedures, psychopathology, social psychology, principles and counseling process, and counseling theory.

· Technical and operational knowledge: Application testing and translation knowledge, communication skills and competence in special intervention procedures.

· Practical training: Extensive training and training to enable counselors to deal with any emergencies.

Additional training in skills development for use in multicultural areas, as well as additional training in specialized counseling areas is also required.

WORKING COUNSELING

Master's degree in mentor education is considered to be the preparation for entry level as a professional. It equips them to work and apply assessment skills and clinical interventions in a variety of settings (schools, agencies, universities) and in a variety of ways (individual, group, and family counseling).

Physician training places as much emphasis on research as it does on performance. This degree is intended to prepare professionals to work independently as academics, administrators, senior physicians, and educators. Doctoral level training is considered a final qualification, meaning that a graduate (after completing an internship and licensing requirements) may be working in an independent position as a manager.

REQUIRED SIGNS

To be effective in their role, counselors must be willing to assist others and to acquire certain qualities and abilities.

Communication Skills

Effective counselors need to have good communication skills. Counselors need to have a natural ability to listen and to be able to express their thoughts and feelings clearly to others. Some of these skills can be developed during graduate school and developed and refined during their career.

Acceptance

Non-judgment and acceptance are essential aspects of any relief work. But professional consultants should be able to "start where the client is." This term is often used in counseling to describe the ability to communicate with clients with an open, non-judgmental attitude - to accept the client for what he or she is in the current situation. Counselors need to be able to convey welcome to their clients with warmth and understanding.

Empathy

Counselors help people through difficult and stressful times in their lives. They must be able to show empathy - the ability to hear what the other person is feeling. Empathy means that you can really imagine what it is like to stand in someone else's shoes. Compassion and compassion help clients feel understood and heard.

Problem Solving Skills

It is not for the consultant to solve customer problems, but counselors must have excellent problem-solving skills to be able to help their clients identify and make changes in negative thinking and other risky behaviors that may have an impact on their affairs.

Reporting Skills

Counselors need to have a strong set of interpersonal skills to help establish faster relationships with clients and build stronger relationships. They should give their undivided attention to the customers and be able to develop trust. Counselors need to be able to focus all their attention on what their clients are saying and to avoid being distracted by their own problems or concerns while in session.

Flexibility

Adaptation to counseling is defined as the ability to adapt and change the way the counselor responds to meet the needs of clients. The counselor does not remain firm and adheres to a pre-determined treatment plan where clients need a different approach. Flexibility is one of the most important qualities of a qualified counselor.

Self-awareness

Self-awareness is the ability to look inward and identify the needs and desires of a person that can be met, such as the need for intimacy or the desire to be competent in the workplace. This feature prevents consultant issues from interfering with or conflict with those of your clients.

Different Cultural Skills

Counselors help people from all walks of life. They must demonstrate multiculturalism which means that the counselor seeks to relate and understand clients regardless of their race, nationality, religious or political beliefs or economic background.

HEAVENLY NEWS.

The method of counseling changes into counseling, coaching, coaching, consultation, etc. as the modern generation emerges.

Training is the latest development from three main streams:

1) Psychotherapy and counseling 2) Business consultation and organizational development 3) Personal development training. In addition it focuses on areas such as social science, psychology, good adult development, career counseling, counseling and other forms of counseling, and sharing similarities with other fields, such as organizational consultation, management development, and training. It works on the philosophy of people limiting themselves and closing their beliefs and destructive patterns.

Counseling is a process in which a knowledgeable person gives advice, support, encouragement to an inexperienced person. A mentor is a teacher or mentor who leads with guidance and example. The Adviser provides guidance, wisdom, knowledge and support on how the ward can find and benefit from it. It is a model of health education based on the goal of a more experienced counselor. The need and usability of a mentor is now widely recognized in all areas, especially in educational institutions and corporate organizations. To help the instructor build confidence in the individual and build self-confidence, the counselor often asks questions and challenges the counselor while giving guidance and encouragement.

A professional consultant who provides advice in a particular area of expertise such as law, administration, medicine, etc. The consultant is usually an expert in the field with extensive knowledge of the subject. Provides advice to potential clients or companies in a particular field or specialty.

The term training refers to the acquisition of knowledge, skills, and abilities as a result of the teaching of job skills or practical skills as well as knowledge related to specific useful skills.

FUNCTIONS

Career guidance has been a key element of the premature leadership movement and included helping each person to choose the right calling. Career counseling is about maturing one's career within the development field. With this, the counselor devises intervention strategies to help his or her client. The mentor, both at the primary and secondary level, appears as a student advisor and a mentor to teachers, parents and administrators. As a student counselor he helps solve problems for a few students and as a mentor he is able to help many students by consulting teachers, parents and administrators, thus developing sensitivity to teacher problems and deepening their understanding of student behavior and activities and initiating them. in basic student guidance skills. This enhances the scope of the counselor's ad performance helps to provide a student body, leading to desirable goals such as better school performance and greater reduction of moral and ethical issues.

ACTIVITIES ARE IMPORTANT

The duties of a counselor can be summarized as follows:

1. Identify areas of problem or difficulty for individuals, their strengths and limitations.

2. Helping people to understand themselves and their aspects of the situation as fully as possible.

3. To help develop the skills of individuals with greater self-awareness, so that they can make full use of natural resources.

4. Reduce suffering, reach for appropriate solutions, make responsible decisions and thus allow customers to become more realistic.

PICTURES

Both counselors and counselors bring to counseling relationships the most important principles affecting education, employment, marriage and family affairs, as well as individual responsibilities and obligations of those around them and those in their position as an obligation. citizen.

Price issues become critical in the counseling system where (i) the advisor and advisor prices are different and (ii) the advisor prices cause some difficulty in his or her area. The counselor must keep in mind that the general purpose of the procedure is to help the client help himself. Therefore, the counselor needs to help the client discuss its values in the client's own environment, and help the client solve the difficulty or deal with the situation in an effective way. It is important that you do not force the advisor's standards on the client.

TEST

The practice of assessment includes the collection of information to identify, analyze, evaluate and correct problems, problems, and clients' situations in a relationship relationship. Evaluation is used as a basis for problem identification, planning interventions, evaluation and / or customer evaluation, and client and stakeholder information. Many beginner counselors may make the mistake of identifying a test as a means of reaching a conclusion, such as providing a label or diagnosing a client. Testing is often seen as an important process in all aspects of counseling. Whether you are practicing at school, doing self-employment, agency, or other health care settings, testing plays an important role. Testing goes beyond step management. Testing involves identifying statements,
actions, and processes to help individuals, groups, couples, and families improve in the area of counseling. While consultants have the opportunity to reduce the scope of their practice regarding client processes, ideas, and types, the consultant will not be able to work without understanding the evaluation processes and procedures in counseling.

There is a difference between testing and testing. Assessment focuses on collecting information; exploration refers to the measurement of psychological structures using the tools or processes mentioned. In this sense, the element means the event that is present but which cannot be directly detected. For example, variables such as height and weight can be seen directly. Length and weight measurement systems are available to minimize errors and ensure the accuracy of the results. However, not all variables can be directly detected. Emotional conditions such as depression or happiness, or psychological factors such as intelligence, or even attitudes such as depression, cannot be directly detected or measured. Construction may not be easily seen. In addition, construction may vary, depending on the performance description - how construction is measured.

The testing process, and sometimes testing, is needed to understand the client. However, the distinction between assessment and assessment may be regarded as an academic activity. In general, these terms may change, as the testing process (i.e., managing, scoring, and translating a tool) cannot be separated from the testing process. Therefore, testing is part of testing. A distinction is made between standard and non-standard tests. General testing refers to a formal system in which a specific set of rules and guidelines related to governance, points, and interpretations are consistently followed to ensure accurate results at a particular time and in all nations. Standardized testing involves tools developed under a rigorous process and produces results that may be demographic or meaningful to the individual in a demographic context. Tools like Success Test, Fitness Test, and Personal Testing fit this definition. Unconventional testing refers to the process of gathering information without complying with a strict set of rules or guidelines. Rare tests may include clinical discussions. Even if those discussions follow a particular pattern or pattern, deviations from management occur due to the personal nature of the interaction and address of the client's personal needs. Such experiments may not adhere to strict control, score points, and the translation process.

BODY STATUS

ROOM

Counseling can happen anywhere but a certain type of physique may encourage and improve the counseling process better than others. Benjamin

(1987) and Shertzer and Stone (1980) emphasize that among the most important factors influencing a counseling program is the place where counseling takes place. Although there is no universal quality that the room should have certain comfortable conditions inside the room where counseling will be provided it can provide a good environment for both the counselor and the counselor. Ideal atmosphere includes a room with quiet colors, light that is not too bright and not too bright or too dim and stressful, with no clutter with comfortable, comfortable furniture and good ventilation. It should be free of external disturbances and emit a feeling of warmth. In short it should be comfortable for a relaxed atmosphere where the client can communicate in a relaxed atmosphere.

The order of sitting inside the room depends on the advisor. Some counselors prefer to sit behind a desk. However it has been established that the desk can be a physical and figurative barrier against the development of the relationship between the client and the counselor. Benjamin (1987) suggests that counselors can install two chairs and a table nearby in the area. Seats can be 90 degree angles from each other so clients can look to their advisors or move forward. Counselors can choose another variety of physical arrangements according to their level of comfort.

The distance between the mentor and the client (local features) can affect the relationship. A range of 30 to 39 inches was found as a measure of the comfort distance between the counselor and the client of both sexes. This large distance can vary in room size and furniture layout. Benjamin (1987) and Shertzer and Stone (1980) emphasize that regardless of the arrangement within the room, it is a universal requirement that counselors not be distracted when conducting times. All calls must be intercepted. If possible, counselors should make sure that you do not disturb the door to prevent others from entering. Listening and visual privacy is endorsed by professional ethics codes and ensures extensive client disclosure.

LENGTH OF LESSON

During individual counseling sessions the session will take approximately 50-

minutes. This 50-55 minute is called the "cure hour." This is a common practice, although some doctors will offer 45-minute sessions or 60-minute sessions. A 50-55 minute session and “closing” session will help the counselor gather his thoughts, take notes (if they did not take them during the session), and 'reset' them before his next client enters. office. The counselor may also need to stretch and relax between sessions. In some cases, the counselor may recommend a longer session (such as 80-85 minutes). It is difficult to get a medical job in a short time

GROUP ADVICE

Group counseling offers some benefits of working with a variety of people, as groups can be formed to meet the needs of children, adolescents, young people, middle-aged and older people.

The following are the goals and objectives of the groups:

- Growing in self-acceptance and learning not to be perfect.
- Learning how to trust yourself and others.
- Promoting self-awareness and the development of unique self-awareness.
- Reduce fear of intimacy, and learn to reach those you want love to be close to.
- Deviate from meeting the expectations of others, and set your own standards we can live by.
- Increasing self-awareness, and increasing opportunities for choice and action.
- Be careful to choose and make wise decisions.
- Highly sensitive to the needs and feelings of others.
- Defining values and determining how, and how, to convert them.
- Finding ways to understand, and solve personal problems.

Team building

In building a team, the first step is to clarify its purpose. It is a good idea to give more time to planning, because if planning is not done well, and if members are not well selected and well prepared, teams may fail to achieve their goal.

The way a group is advertised affects the way in which members can be found, as well as the types of people who will join the group. Contacting a potential member is one of the best ways to hire members. A leader can, by personal contact, enthusiastically demonstrate that a group has a potential value to someone.

The group leader conducts a pre-team interview with each potential member for evaluation and guidance. He then selects team members whose needs and goals are in line with the group's established policies, which will not hinder the group's process, and their well-being will not compromise the team's experience.
In choosing members of a particular group, there are some basic factors to keep in mind.

1. How big should the team be?

The appropriate size of a group depends on the age of the members, the mentor's knowledge as a leader, the type and purpose of the group, and whether there is a leader or partner. For example, a group with elementary school children may be limited to four or five members, whereas a group of teenagers may be eight to ten. The group should be large enough to provide ample opportunity for discussion, and be small enough for everyone to feel involved in the group.

2. How often should the group meet, and for how long?

For children and young children, short meetings are always a good time to pay close attention. If a group is running a school, meeting times may coincide with scheduled classroom times. For a group of active adults, a two-hour weekly session may be better. The frequency and duration of the meeting should be in line with your leadership style and the type of people in the group.

3. Where should the group meet?

Physical preparation and team environment contribute to, or interfere with, the team's climate. Privacy and freedom from disruption are essential. Party leaders sometimes think that meeting outside is a good way to promote order, but often such a situation is not secretive and a source of frustration.

4. Will the membership be voluntary or automatic?

While it is good to have a group formed only for those who want to be part of the team, some groups include clients who need to be present. Going to a team because instructed by someone else greatly reduces the chances of success. The key to effective participation lies in carefully guiding members, preparing them to be part of the team, and in believing the leader that the team process has something to offer potential members.

5. Should the group be opened or closed?

An open group is one that is characterized by a change in membership, while a closed group does not add new members during the life of the group. Closed groups have some distinct advantages, as trust can be enhanced and work accomplished. If membership changes every week, as in other open groups, it may be difficult to accomplish productive work as a team.

Once members have been tested, and the group has been formed, it is helpful to conduct a first or pre-group session with all selected members. A pre-team meeting can be an extension of the individual assessment process, as it is a great way to present basic information, help members get to know each other, and help them decide whether to commit to the group or not. Depending on the nature of the group, certain basic rules will need to be established in advance.

GRADE 1 PROCESS PHASE:

In the early stages, the intermediate process involves guidance and evaluation. During this time, members get to know each other, learn how the team works, develop verbal and unspecified behaviors that govern group behavior, discuss fears and expectations about the group, articulate their expectations, identify personal goals, and determine how safe the group is. to them. One of the best ways to create a climate of trust is for the leader to encourage members to openly express any feelings of mistrust, or lack of trust they may have. If the work is to continue, mistrust must first be seen, and then dealt with by the group. Otherwise, the hidden agenda grows, mistrust is expressed in indirect ways, and the party stops progressing.

Helping Members Explain Terms

One of the tasks in the first phase of a team leader is to help members set their own goals. Some members often come to a group with vague and clear goals, for example, 'I just want to be able to communicate with others,' or 'I hope I will be able to communicate with my feelings.' These vague ideas need to be translated into specific and practical terms. Limit some expressions, e.g., _I would like to learn to express my feelings. 'The leader might ask, _What other emotions do you find difficult to express? Whom do you have problems with expressing your feelings? In what situations do you find it difficult to express yourself? How would you like to be different? 'Creating contracts, verbally and in writing, can help its members have tangible principles that guide their participation in the team.

Phase 2: Transformation Phase

Features of the Transformation Phase

Some groups remain trapped in the transition phase, because resistance passes or conflict is ignored or transmitted. At this stage of the group's emergence, feelings of anxiety and resentment are common, and members tend to:

· Being concerned about what they think of them when they open
up, like that
involved in the acceptance or rejection of another.

· Assessing the leader and other members, to find out how safe the environment is.

· Struggling and wanting to play safely, or the danger of going beyond safety once if affected.

· Gaining a struggle for control and power. Conflict between members, and between members and leaders, it is normal.

· Being challenged to learn how to work against conflict.

Hesitation is fully involved in solving personal problems, because they are not sure that others will take care of you.

Anxiety

Anxiety grows in fear of letting others see us as superior to what society sees. Anxiety is also caused by the fear of being judged and misunderstood, ranging from the need for additional structure, to a lack of clarity about the expected values, norms and behaviors in the group. As participants begin to trust other members and leader more, they become more and more able to share with others, and this openness reduces their anxiety by allowing others to see them as they really are.

Common Fear Related to Resistance

If fear is kept inside, then all sorts of avoidances happen. While group leaders will not force members to discuss fears that may hinder their participation, leaders can empathetically invite members to address this fear. Fear often includes fear of making a fool of yourself, fear of rejection, fear of being hanged, fear of not liking what you have found, fear of exposing yourself, fear of being attacked and being left unprotected. , and fear of getting close to others. It is important for the group leader to understand, and appreciate the concerns and resilience of the members. Resistance should be respected, as members are expected to have doubts, doubts, and fears. The primary function of a leader at this time is to help members recognize, and deal with, their resistance to self-defense from anxiety.

Learning to Recognize and Deal With Conflict

The stage of change is characterized by conflict, and the expression of negative emotions. Members challenge other members and leader. Some of the statements that show the conflict between the members are, 'Why do we focus so much on the evil in this group?' 'I feel threatened by Ms. X.'

Disagreements with leaders are rarely in the transition phase, because the main function of the members is to learn how to challenge the leader in a positive and constructive way. This could be a sign that members are moving towards independence. How a leader handles this challenge is crucial to the future of the group. When leaders are overly defensive, and refuse to accept criticism, they prevent members from treating each other in a positive way, thus undermining trust within the party.

At this stage of team growth, the leader's main task is to help members move from conflict to a level of openness. Some activities are:

• educating members on the importance of recognizing and dealing with conflict;
• teach them to respect and cooperate with their resistance; to provide a model for members by directly addressing any challenges they face; and encourage members to express their reaction to what is happening within the group.

Stage 3: Performance Phase

In the first stage, the group is characterized by experimentation, as members discover what the group is all about and their place in it. During the transition, there is an expression of feelings about the interaction between the group, as well as individual problems. The performance phase is reflected in the members' commitment to assessing key issues they bring to the sessions.

One of the key features of the action stage is for participants to learn how to get involved in group work, rather than waiting for an invitation to participate. In a sense, there is a sharing of team leadership responsibilities, because members are able to take greater responsibility for the work being done in the group.

An important feature of the working stage is team cohesion, which results in members being willing to go public with each other. Other indicators of the level of solidarity (or 'unity') in the group, the level of cooperation between team members, the level of initiation shown by participants, the arrival rates, punctuality, the level of trust shown, and the level of support, encouragement, and care that members show in their interactions.

The unity of the group and the genuine constructive feelings within the group occur after the negative emotions are identified and expressed, because expressing negative emotions is one of the ways to test the group's freedom and integrity. Participants soon found that the group was a safe haven from disagreements, and that they were still welcome despite their negative feelings. Solidarity occurs when participants open their mouths and pose a risk by making themselves known. Solidarity, which is the process of solidarity, and genuine trust, are the things that a group achieves by committing itself to being honest. At this point members are able to see common problems, and they are impressed by the consistency of the news.

Phase 4: The Final Phase

During the final phase many factors can be expected, all of which are associated with the successful completion of a complex integration and termination process. These include the possibility of grief, anxiety about the reality of the breakup, the tendency of members to retreat and participate in less sensitive ways in anticipation of the end of the group, concerns about one's ability to apply it in daily life. what one has learned from the group, and decisions about what steps to take, and app development. Subsequent meetings or feedback programs may also be discussed, so members can be encouraged to make their own change plans.

The final stages of team flexibility are important, because during this time members have the opportunity to clarify the meaning of their team experience, combine their gains, and review their decisions about what new behaviors they want to convey. daily life.

As team members realize that their team is coming to an end, there is a risk that they will begin to distance themselves from the team experience, and fail to consider how their learning in the team might have an impact outside of the group. behavior. Other problems that occur during this time include the tendency for some members to refrain from updating their knowledge, as well as failing to incorporate it into a specific cognitive framework, thereby limiting the application of what they have learned in their daily lives. In addition, members may view the group as an end in itself rather than an interactive learning laboratory. For these reasons, team leaders must learn to help participants put a positive view of what happened in the group.

Tracking and Evaluation

A follow-up meeting can be held a few months after the end of the group, assessing the impact of the group on each member. Such a session is a way to increase the chances of members getting a lasting benefit from what is happening in the group. Many people report that just knowing that they will be reunited as a team in the future, after the dissolution of the group, is what motivates them to stick to their commitment to making their plans work.

XV

SLAB V: (Conclusion) STAGES OF COUNSELLING & PROFESSIONAL TECHNIQUES

The counseling process is usually defined by a sequence of interactions or steps. The counseling process involves the establishment of relationships, followed by a client problem identification method and assessment patterns, which lead to problem planning and finalization through action and termination. A brief description of each of these categories is provided in the following paragraphs.

Build Relationships

Relationship counseling. It is also described as a supportive relationship. Therefore, it follows that if it is to be a useful relationship, the counselor must take the first step in the interview to establish an attitude based on trust, mutual respect, open and free communication, and a general understanding of that counsel. the process involves. Although the burden is increasingly changing for the client, at this stage the responsibility for the counseling process is far greater than that of the counselor. The counselor uses techniques designed to relieve tension, anxiety, stress and open communication. Both the mentor's attitude and verbal communication are essential to developing a satisfying relationship. All verbal communication skills counselors are used. This includes careful listening, understanding and feeling with the client. The level of client-client relationships influences the outcomes of the counseling process.

The various factors that are important in establishing this counseling client relationship are good looks, respect, accurate empathy and honesty. These conditions mean the ease of the counselor, which is the ability to understand and get along with the client, as well as the client's evaluation. Client-client relationships not only help increase the likelihood of clients reaching their goals but also become a potential model for positive interpersonal relationships, which can be used by clients to improve the quality of their other relationships without medical treatment. Counselors should keep in mind that the purpose of a counseling relationship is to meet the needs of clients as much as possible and not the needs of counselors. The counseling process within these relationships seeks to assist the client in taking responsibility for their problem and its solution. This will be facilitated by the consultant's communication skills, the ability to identify and express customer feelings, and the ability to identify and obtain information about clients' concerns and needs. Establishing a relationship with a client should be achieved at the beginning of the counseling process, as this will usually determine whether the client will continue or not.

The first counseling process has a goal and the client has a goal. The principles of the first counseling process are as follows: 1) Build good and comfortable relationships. 2) Explain the counseling process and similar obligations to the client. 3) Adjust connection. 4) Identify and confirm customer concerns you have brought to seek counseling assistance. 5) Arrange, with the client, to obtain the test data needed to proceed with the counseling process. Understand the counseling process and its responsibilities in the program. Share and expand reasons for seeking advice. Collaborate on exploring both the problem and you.

Problem Diagnosis and Evaluation

Once enough relationships have been established, clients will be more receptive to in-depth discussion and concerns that worry them. At this stage, clients should bear the brunt of the burden because it is their problem, therefore, it is their responsibility to pass on the problem to the counselor and answer any questions the counselor may have to extend the help and assistance of counselors. During this phase, the counselor continues to demonstrate the behavior of the visitor and may emphasize communication skills such as summarizing, clarifying doubts, seeing, evaluating or providing feedback. The counselor may ask the client, but the questions are explained in a way that helps the client to further assess the client's problem area. Questions that may embarrass clients are avoided. Throughout this phase the counselor should be extremely careful about knowing the cultural differences and cultural contexts and responses. Here, the counselor seeks to distinguish between more problems and deeper and more complex problems. The counselor tries to determine if the problem mentioned at the outset is a real problem or if there may be another fundamental issue that needs to be addressed and addressed by the client. This can be a time for information collection. The more knowledgeable a consultant has, the greater the likelihood of an accurate assessment of customer needs. The information is grouped into three categories: duration, intensity and intensity of the brain are as follows: i) Duration: This includes past clients, especially those who might view them as influencing their lives. ii) Emotional sensitivity: This includes the feelings and feelings of the client about himself or herself, as well as other important ones, including groups, attitudes, values, and self-esteem. iii) Mental acuity: This includes the client's problem-solving skills, coping styles, the common sense used to make daily decisions and client strength and readiness to learn.

The goal of this section is for counselors to seek out and gather as much information as possible from the client. The counselor also shares these ideas with the client. The goal of this phase is for the counselor and client to see the problem and its solution. One of the goals of the counselor in this phase is to help the client understand themselves that he / she sees the need to address the need for change and practice. Troubleshooting is used to promote customer understanding of problem-solving strategies. The steps or stages of problem identification and evaluation are as follows: 1) Define the problem by clearly identifying the problem. 2) Assess the problem by gathering the necessary information and exploring alternatives to finding a solution to the problem. 3) Consolidate the information collected from the client and summarize and lay it out clearly so that steps can be taken to resolve the issue.

Plan Problem Solving

Once the counselor has determined that all the important information about a client's concerns is available and understandable, and once the client has accepted the need to do something about a particular problem, it is time to make a plan to resolve or resolve the problem. of the client. Here, setting effective goals becomes an integral part of the counseling process. Mistakes in setting goals can lead to unproductive counseling processes and clients losing confidence in the counseling process. At this stage there are a number of steps in looking at the processes involved. 1) Explain the problem 2) Identify and list all possible solutions 3) Check the results of the suggested solutions. 4) Prioritize solutions based on basic needs. In the ongoing development of this program, the counselor realizes that the client will often not come to the basic ideas, impacts, or possibilities as quickly as the counselor will approach. However, most counselors will agree that it is better to guide the client towards achieving this understanding itself, rather than just telling the client directly. To facilitate customer understanding, the counselor can use repetitive techniques, eye contact, translation, information and explicit encouragement.

Application for Solution and Termination

In this last step, the bonds are clearly cut. The client is responsible for implementing the fixed solution, and the counselor is responsible for encouraging the client to do something about the solution to their fixed problem. At a time when the client is actively encouraged to apply the solution to the problem, the counselor will usually keep in touch as a source of follow-up, support and encouragement. The patient may also need the help of a counselor when things go awry. Once it has been determined that the counselor and the client handle the client's case as well as possible, the process should be terminated.

Deletion is the job of the consultant, although the client can cut times at any time. The counselor usually gives some kind of indication that the next interview should be completed and may conclude by summarizing the key points of the counseling process. Usually, the counselor leaves the door open so that the client can return to a situation where additional help is needed. Since counseling is a learning process, the counselor hopes that the client has not only learned to deal with a particular problem, but also learned problem-solving skills that will reduce the likelihood that clients will need additional counseling in the future.

WORK METHODS

There are many different strategies that counselors can use with their clients. Here are some suggestions on how to look or get an appointment for appointments:

Areas of Influence: This assessment tool will enable a person to look at aspects of his or her health and see which areas may be influential and influential in them. It is man's job to discover what plans in his life are giving him strength, and what pressures are putting him under pressure. Other areas of influence that need to be considered are: themselves, immediate family, friends, spouse, extended family, work or school, community, culture or religion, and any external influences.

Definition: The counselor should ask his client to clarify what he is telling him to make sure he understands the situation. This will help the counselor to avoid any misconceptions or to avoid making any assumptions that might impede his response.

Client Expectations: When a person enters treatment, they should express their views about the counseling and their beliefs about treatment. Initially, they should be able to contact their counselor about what they expect to get from counseling. This can help the counselor to direct and direct their counsel accordingly.

Controversy: This does not mean that the client is dealing with a therapist, or vice versa. The conflict that should occur here is within the client. The patient should be able to self-examine during counseling. However, the speed at which they do this should be discussed between the counselor and the client.

Congress: This has to do with the counselor being honest about his or her response and beliefs about his or her client's status and progress. The more truthful and truthful they are in their counsel, the more their client and hard work to grow and benefit from their help.

Core Conditions: This method of counseling extends to other important aspects that counselors need to incorporate in order to be effective counselors, namely: good judgment, empathy, agreement or integrity, and warmth.

Encouragement: Encouragement is a client-counselor is an important way to help build confidence and respect between the two stakeholders. This process requires the counselor to focus on the strengths and assets of the client to help him or she feels better. This will help in the furtherance of the client.

Involvement: As a therapist, having a good, yet the working relationship with the client is important. However, there will be difficult times in counseling sessions, which will require influential interactions on behalf of the counselor.

Focusing: This process involves the counselor demonstrating that he or she understands what his or her client is going through by using non-judgmental attention without words. Focusing can help the counselor determine what the client needs next in their services.

Urgency: This process involves a counselor who speaks openly about what is happening in the present moment. This helps the client learn what is happening in their real life and apply it in their response to other past situations.

Listening Skills: In any relationship, listening skills are needed to show that the counselor understands and interprets the information his or her client provides in the right way. The consultant should do this by showing attentive listening in non-verbal ways, such as: summarizing, compiling, or comparing their clients' body language.

Open-ended Questions: Open-ended questions encourage people in counseling sessions to provide more information about their discussion. Therefore, these types of questions are used as a way for consultants to help their clients answer how, why, and what.

Summary: This process will show clients that the counselor has listened to their information and considered what he or she has been telling them. Summarizing is good for repeating or clarifying any inaccurate information that may have happened.

Searching for a Good Legacy: The straightforward approach used by mentors helps clients think of their positive strengths and qualities to make them feel strong about themselves.

Emotional Expressions: Counselors use this process to show their clients that they are fully aware of the feelings their client is experiencing. They can do this by using specific words and phrases that their client says to them. Miracle Question: This kind of question-and-answer method will help the client to see the world differently or from a different perspective. A miraculous question could be something related to: — What would your world look like if a miracle happened? What would that miracle be, and how would it turn out? ”

Stages of Change: By assessing client needs, the counselor can determine the changes that need to happen to their client, and when they should occur. This can be determined by what they believe to be the most important thing.

Loyalty: A counselor should create a situation for their client so that their client feels empowered to trust their mentor. The therapist should be: cohesive, warm, empathetic, and speak positively about his or her client.

Capping: Most counselors use a measurement method during their sessions. Capping involves changing the way a conversation turns from emotional to psychological when a counselor feels that their client's feelings need to be silenced or controlled.

Working Alliance: Creating a cooperative partnership between their mentor and their client is essential for a successful counseling environment that works to meet the needs of the client. This process involves the client and therapist becoming active participants during counseling and agreeing on the desired treatment goals, as well as how to achieve those goals.

Proxemics: This process enables the counselor to learn the movement of the space and the communication conditions displayed by their client. By studying the physical condition of their clients, a counselor can determine their feelings, emotions, and reactions.

Disclosure: The counselor will record when personal information is disclosed in certain medical settings. This process will help the counselor learn more about the client and use this information for personal gain only.

Planning: When that person enters counseling, the counselor should discuss the day's agenda with his or her client, activities, and procedures. This method of counseling will help the client understand the mentor's thoughts on deciding how the process will work for them. Soon, the client will get used to the routine, and this creates comfort and confidence in the advice.

Negotiation: This process involves the counselor assessing the level of needs of his client based on the progress he is making. The needs they will face are physical needs, safety needs, love and personal needs, self-confidence needs, and automatic needs. All of this will determine whether a change in counseling should occur.

EGAN Model

Egan Model is a 3-step model or framework provided by Egan as useful in helping people solve problems and improve opportunities. The principles of using the model are to help people 'manage their problems in life more efficiently and develop opportunities that are not fully utilized', and 'to help people become better at helping themselves in their daily lives.' This model emphasizes empowerment. And the personal agenda is central, and the model wants to move the person into action that leads to the results they choose and appreciate.

This model is not based on a particular theory of human development, or on the theory of how problems develop. It is a framework for considering a support process and is best used in working with current and current issues. Like any model, it provides a map, which can be used for testing, but which is not the location itself.. The model can be used and should be used flexibly. The model works best when it comes to Rogers' 'main conditions', assistants talking to the speaker based on truth, respect, and empathy, and if the principles of active listening carefully are always remembered.

The Egan model aims to help the speaker answer 3 key questions:

1. 'What is happening?'
2. 'What do I want instead?'
3. 'How can I get what I want?'

Not everyone needs to answer all 3 questions, and sometimes people can move

return to previous responses. The skilled assistant will work with the speaker in all or in any of the sections, and step back and forth, accordingly.

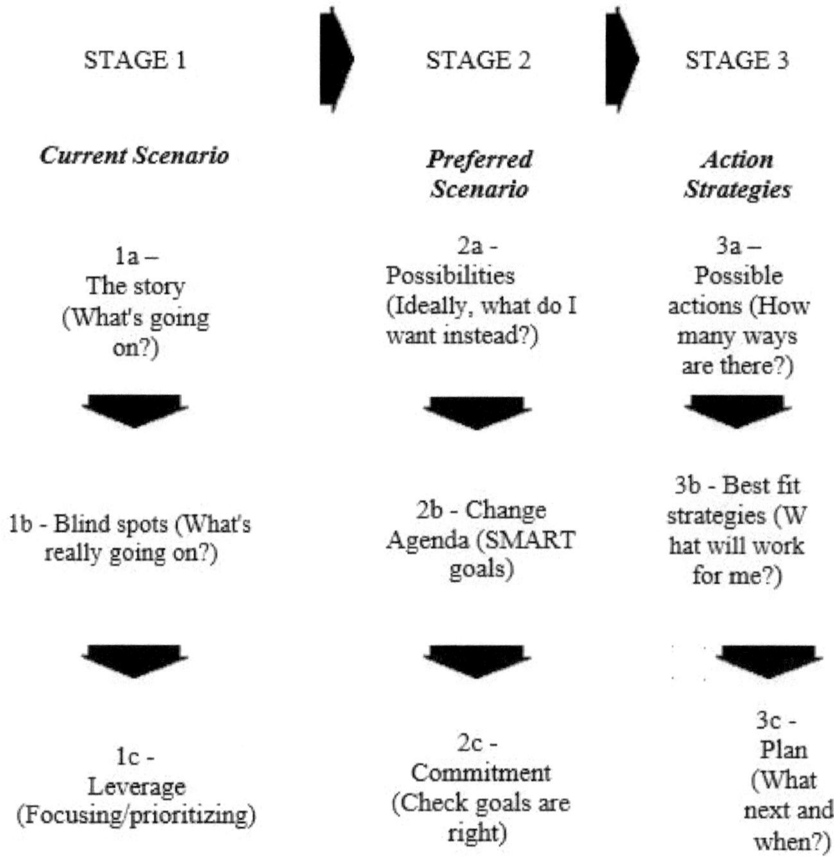

Action Leading to Valued Outcomes

SECTION 1 - What's going on?

Section 1 is about providing a safe environment for the client to tell their story in their own way, and to be fully heard and accepted. It is about a space where one can hear and understand one's story. It's about helping them gently lift their heads to see the wider picture and other ideas, and find a point where they can move on with hope.

1a - large part

The facilitator encourages the client to tell their story, and by using good listening skills actively and demonstrates key situations, helps them to explore and unravel the myth, and to meditate. For some, that is enough, for others it is just the beginning.

Skills in Section 1a: - Active listening, reflection, summarizing, comprehension testing, open-ended questions, summarizing.

Helpful Questions: How do you feel / do you feel about that? What did you think / thought? How was that / was that for you? Keep it open! What else is there about that?

1b - the challenging part

In this case, it may be difficult for the speaker to see clearly, or in a variety of ways. With the help of empathy and challenges, the speaker reveals areas of blindness or gaps in their perceptions and assessment of the situation, to others and to themselves - their patterns, the impact of their behavior on the situation, their strengths. "I never thought about how I would feel from a colleague's point of view."

• **Skills:** Challenging; different ideas, patterns and communications, appropriate and appropriate, negative self-expression, blind areas (disagreements, distortions, incomplete awareness, things said, unspoken), identity, specific details, power.

• **Helpful Questions:**

o How do others see you?

o Is there anything you are not paying attention to? o How do you think / feel?

o What can he say about all this?

o What about all this problem for you? o What is another way to look at it?

1c -Focus and focus

People often feel trapped; that's why they want to talk. At this stage, the facilitator seeks to remove the client from feeling overwhelmed by helping them choose a place where they can move forward, which can make a difference and benefit them. "I now see an important area in which to start my relationship with K"

• **Skills:** Encouraging focus and prioritizing work.

• **Helpful Questions:**

o What is the most important of all these? o What could be better to work on now?

o What can make the difference? o What is controllable?

SECTION 2 - What do I want instead?

People often move from problem to action, or problem to solution, without thinking about what they really want, or how their problems can be opportunities. Section 2 is about this, helping the speaker open up a picture of what we really want, and how things can get better. This phase is crucial in producing strength and hope.

2a - creative part

The facilitator helps the speaker to think about his or her appropriate position; 'if you could wake up tomorrow with everything you wish, like your beautiful world, what would it be like?' The speaker is encouraged to increase their attention span and to focus on positive things rather than on what might have been. For some people this is scary, for others it is liberating. "At first it was very difficult but after a while I thought and started to be very happy with what we can achieve in the department."

• **Skills:** Thinking, making it easier to think thoughtfully, i.e. o Quantity vs. Quality Anything that goes - have fun

o Write down ideas and words verbally, do not analyze or judge o Keep saying - 'what else?'

o Don't rush, allow more time

• **Helpful Questions:**

o What do you want instead? o What will happen?
o What are you doing / thinking / feeling?
o What would you have that you do not have now?
o What if it was better / a little better?

2b - part of the practical test

From the creative and theoretical dialogue, the speaker develops goals that are specific, measurable, achievable / relevant (to them, in their own context), realistic (referring to the real world), and have an attached time, i.e. SMART goals. Tough but unattainable goals are encouraging.

"It sounds good to be clear that I want to get along well with my colleagues about our rules and obligations."

• **Skills:** to facilitate selective and practical assessment of internal and external geography.

• **Helpful Questions:**

o What exactly is your goal?
o How will you know when you get there?

o What can you carry / gain? o Which is best for you?

o In all of this, what could be more real? o When do you want to achieve it?

2c - forward

This section aims to assess the validity of the goal before taking action, as well as to help the client evaluate their commitment to the goal by reviewing its costs and benefits of achieving it. Is it worth it? "Sounds dangerous but I have to solve this."

• **Skills:** simplifying cost and benefit assessments, and evaluating goal commitment.

• **Helpful Questions:**

o What will be the benefits if you get this?

o How will it be different for you once you have done this?

o What will be the cost of doing this? Any disadvantages / disadvantages of doing this?

Stage 3 - How do I get there?

This is the 'that' phase ... how will one go beyond the goals identified in Section 2? It is about possible strategies and actions, about doing something to get started, while considering what / who can help and prevent making a change.

3a - another creative component!

The speaker is helped to integrate strategies - 101 ways to achieve the goal - and by encouraging and encouraging you to think more deeply. What people, places, ideas, organizations can help? The purpose is to free the person to produce new and different ideas for action, to come out of the old ideas. "There were treasures that may have come from ideas that seemed crazy."

• **Skills:** Encouraging dialogue

• **Helpful Questions:**

o How many different ways to do this? o Who / what can help?

o What has worked in the past / in others? o What about the opposite ideas?

3b - focus on appropriate strategies

What in the discussion can be chosen as a practical strategy for the speaker, in their circumstances, in line with their values? Forcefield analysis can be used here to look at what internal and external factors (individuals and organizations) may be helpful and prevent action and how they can be strengthened or weakened respectively. "I would feel free to try to talk to him about how he sees things."

· **Section 3b skills:** Promoting truth choice and evaluation.

· **Helpful Questions:**

o Which of these ideas is most appealing? o What is likely to work for you?
o What is within your resources / control?

3c - to action

The purpose is to help the client plan the next steps. The strategy is divided into pieces of action equivalent to biting. Here the client does almost all the work, producing its own application. The facilitator works with them to turn good intentions into specific programs with time constraints. While encouraging, it is also important not to push the speaker to do things to please the assistant. "I will make sure we have time together before the end of the month. I will book a meeting, so that we can be sure that there will be a quiet and uninterrupted time. I will arrange this before Friday."

· **Skills:** Encouraging action planning.

· **Helpful Questions:**

o What will you do first? What? o What will you do next? What?

Once the decision-making process has been reached, the information to try it out can be the start of a mentoring / training follow-up session. Work was about to start in the first phase again, I told a new story. If the app was not accessible, that is fine, and the model can be used in a series of times.

The key to using a model, like any theory or model, is to keep the agenda of the speakers central, individual in front and theory behind, and applying the model to the individual, rather than the opposite.

DISCUSSION

Counseling interviews are a common form of communication. The counselor takes on the role of counselor whenever he or she is called upon to provide counsel on emotional, financial, educational, or personal problems. These conditions are very important as they directly affect the critical aspects of the lives of others. Effective counseling skills begin with a self-assessment of the counselor's feelings and communication skills Based on this analysis, the counselor should be realistic about his or her counseling skills and not try to solve all the problems encountered. The counselor should also consider the client's background so that the counselor's advice can meet that person's needs.

Based on the counselor's analysis of the individual's abilities and needs, the counselor must decide whether to use the direct or indirect method. The guidance method is best if the counselor is required to control the interview situation and the indirect method is the best way where the interviewer can better manage the situation. Although the structure of the interview may vary, four stages are often followed. First, a mentor should build a relationship and create a conducive climate. Second, he should carefully assess the problem / problem the client is facing. Third, the counselor should carefully consider the client's feelings. Finally, the counselor must come to a decision and offer possible solutions.

The right interview environment should allow for trust, openness, and the relationship between the client and the counselor. The counselor must also be an effective listener to truly understand the client's feelings. When appropriate, the counselor should ask inquiry questions in order to gather additional information. The counselor should use a client-focused approach and provide direct or indirect feedback. Somewhat inaccurate answers encourage the interviewer to continue analyzing and conveying ideas. Responses with high-level responses give the interviewer directions and decisions. These types of responses are two continuous conclusions, and can be considered exaggerated. After a successful closing of the interview, the counselor must carefully evaluate the interview in order to continue refining their skills.

TEST

Counselors often use tests to assess, place, and direct and update to help clients develop their self-esteem, practice decision-making, and discover new behaviors. It can be used for a variety of treatments e.g. individual, marriage, group, and family and any customer data collection, assessing the level of other factors, such as stress and anxiety, or measuring customer personality traits.

The steps involved in the process of applying the test to counseling include the following: - selecting a test, administering the test, scoring points, interpreting the results, communicating the results.

Choice: After explaining the purpose of the test, the counselor looks at the various sources to get information about the available tests. Resources include review books, journals, test books, and test and evaluation books (Anastasi, 1988; Cronbach, 1979). The most complete source of information for a particular test is usually a test book.
Management: Test management is often done in the same way as test developers. Manual instructions need to be followed in order to make a valid comparison of each individual school with a standardized assessment team. Individual management issues against the group need to be reconsidered. Clients and the purpose for which they are tested will contribute to decisions regarding group evaluation.

Points:

Scoring scores follow the instructions provided in the test manual, The Adviser is sometimes given the option of the scoring machine rather than scoring by hand. Both the good and the bad aspects of this choice need to be considered. It is generally believed that obtaining test scores is better treated by the machine because it is not biased.

Interpretation:

The interpretation of test results is usually an area that allows for greater flexibility within the testing process. Depending on the Adviser's perspective and the standard of manual testing guidelines, translation may be shorter and more advanced, or there may be more detailed and explicitly based theory (Tinsley & Bradley, 1986). Because this area allows for greater flexibility, and it is a more vulnerable area for misuse. The mentor experience allows for efficient, careful translation of the results.

Communication:

Response to client test results completes the formal testing process. Here, the therapeutic skills of the Advisers are fully functional. The consultant uses verbal and verbal communication skills to convey messages to clients and assess their understanding of that.

NEWS IN THE TEST

Confidentiality:

Ethical and legal limitations on what can be disclosed in counseling apply to the use of testing as well as other confidential information shared between client and counselor. The issue of trust, which is accompanied by confidentiality, is important in all aspects of testing. No information may be shared without a relationship without the full consent of the client. Information is provided to someone outside the relationship only after the information to be used in the test is fully disclosed to the client. This information includes when, where, and to whom it is disclosed. The purpose of the disclosure is also shared with the client and the information will be clearly defined. Confidentiality issues are best discussed with the client before performing any test management. Clients are fully informed, prior to the evaluation, of the matter of confidentiality in respect of the examination who are the most active participants in the counseling process.

Preparing the Advisor:

Tests are only as good as their construction, proper use and adjustment of the advisor you intend to use. The skills and abilities that counselors need or apply the tests in practice: (i) A clear understanding of the intended purpose of the test, (ii) Awareness of the client's needs regarding the test to be performed (iii) Knowledge of the test. testing, its legitimacy, credibility and the general team for which it was built. (iv) Examine yourself before handling it. (v) They have been monitored for monitoring, scoring, interpreting and commenting on the results of the tests to be provided. Supervision of the inspection service delivery function includes all of the above areas of concern. This supervision should be performed by an experienced practitioner in the use of tests in clinical practice.

Preparing a counselor has many aspects and involves developing trainees 'health knowledge, skills and competence. Counseling is a work that can be learned and developed. Most counseling programs recognize that many factors influence the ability to receive counseling. As a result, different types of counselor training and education are available and counseling training may include different aspects of counseling knowledge, awareness, and skill. Counseling training includes independent counseling and training programs, as well as educational qualifications. Doctoral degrees in counselor education and supervision are extended to master's degrees and are designed individually to give emphasis to counseling, guidance, teaching and research. Some people pursue doctoral qualifications to work in colleges and universities to teach and guide future counselors and add to the foundation of research career counseling, while others may pursue doctoral qualifications to advance their career in counseling by assuming administrative and / or administrative roles. in their organizations. In most cases, a person will need to have a master's degree in counseling and work as a counselor before qualifying for a doctorate in education and guidance.

BIBLIOGRAPHY

Corey, G. (1996). Theory and Practice of Counselling and Psychotherapy. 5th ed. Belmount, CA: Brook/Cole.

Nelson, J. (1982). The Theory and Practice of Counselling Psychology. New York: Holt Rinehart & Winston.

Patterson, L.W. & Welfel, E. R. (2000). The Counselling Process. 5th ed. Belmount, CA: Brook/Cole.

Richard Nelson-Jones (2012). Basic Counselling Skills – a Helper's Manual, 3rd Edition, New Delhi: Sage Publication India Pvt Ltd.

Brammer, L.M. & Shostrom, E.L. (1977). Therapeutic Psychology. New Jersey: Englewood Cliffs.

D.John Antony, Skills of Counselling, 2003, Anugraha Publications.

Dudycha, G. J. (1948). A bibliography on careers in psychology: II. *American Psychologist, 3*(12), 543–546.

Foucault, M. (1966/1970). The Order of Things. New York: Vintage.

Ellenberger, H. (1970). The discovery of the unconsciousness. New York: Basic Books.

Foucault, M. (1978). The history of sexuality: An introduction. New York: Vintage.

Young, R. M. (1985). Darwin's metaphor: Nature's place in Victorian culture. Cambridge: Cambridge University Press.

Digby, A. (1985). Madness, morality and medicine: A study of the York Retreat, 1796-1914. Cambridge: Cambridge University Press.

O'Donnell, J. M. (1985). The origins of behaviorism: American psychology, 1870-1920. New York: New York University Press.

Smith, L. D. (1986). Behaviorism and logical positivism: A reassessment of the alliance. Stanford: Stanford University Press.

Richards, R. J. (1987). Darwin and the emergence of evolutionary theories of mind and behavior. Chicago: University of Chicago Press.

Sokal, M. M. (Ed.). (1987). Psychological testing and American society, 1890-1930. New Brunswick: Rutgers University Press.

Morawski, J. G. (Ed.) (1988). The rise of experimentation in American psychology. New Haven: Yale University Press.

Taylor, C. (1989). Sources of the self: The making of the modern identity. Cambridge: Harvard University Press.

Haraway, D. J. (1989). Primate visions: Gender, race, and nature in the world of modern science. New York and London: Routledge.

Danziger, K. (1990). Constructing the subject: Historical origins of psychological research. Cambridge and New York: Cambridge University Press.

Crary, J. (1990). Techniques of the observer: On vision and modernity in the nineteenth century. Cambridge, Mass.: MIT Press.

Clarke, A. and Fujimora, J. (Eds.). (1992). The right tools for the job: At work in twentieth-century life sciences. Princeton: Prince University Press.

Lunbeck, E. (1994). The psychiatric persuasion: Knowledge, gender, and power in modern America. Princeton: Princeton University Press.

Herman, E. (1995). The romance of American psychology: Political culture in the age of experts. Berkeley: University of California Press.

Hacking, I. (1995). Rewriting the soul: Multiple personality and the sciences of memory. Princeton: Princeton University Press.

Cherry, F. (1995). The 'stubborn particulars' of social psychology: Essays on the research process. London and New York: Routledge.

Porter, T. M. (1995). Trust in numbers: The pursuit of objectivity in science and public life. Princeton: Princeton University Press.

Edwards, P. N. (1996) The closed world: Computers and the politics of discourse in Cold War America. Cambridge: MIT Press.

Rose, N. (1996). Inventing our selves: psychology, power, and personhood. Cambridge and New York: Cambridge University Press.

Smith, R. (1997). The Norton history of the human sciences. New York: Norton.

Danziger, K. (1997). Naming the mind: How psychology found its language. London: Sage.

Winter, A. (1998). Mesmerized: Powers of mind in Victorian Britain. Chicago: University of Chicago Press.

Gieryn, T. F. (1999). Cultural boundaries of science: Credibility on the line. Chicago: University of Chicago Press.

Capshew, J. (1999). Psychologists on the march: Science, practice, and professional identity in America, 1929-1969. Cambridge and New York: Cambridge University Press.

Weidman, N. (1999). Constructing scientific psychology: Karl Lashley's mind-brain debates. Cambridge: Cambridge University Press.

Kusch, M. (1999). Psychological Knowledge: A social history and philosophy. New York: Routledge.

Marinelli, L. and Mayer, A. (2002/2003). Dreaming by the Book: Freud's The Interpretation of Dreams and the History of the Psychoanalytic Movement. New York: Other Press.

Dumit, J. (2004). Picturing personhood: Brain scans and biomedical identity. Princeton: Princeton University Press.

Serlin, D. (2004). Replaceable you: Engineering the body in postwar America. Chicago: University of Chicago Press.

Goldstein, J. (2005). The post-revolutionary self: Politics and psyche in France, 1750-1850. Cambridge: Harvard University Press.

Lemov, R. (2005). The world as laboratory: Experiments with mice, mazes, and men. New York: Hill and Wang.

Carson, J. (2007). The measure of merit: Talents, intelligence, and inequality in the French and American republics, 1750-1940. Princeton: Princeton University Press.

Igo, S. E. (2007). The averaged American: Surveys, citizens, and the making of a mass public. Cambridge: Harvard University Press.

Daston, L. and Galison, P. (2007). Objectivity. New York: Zone.

Harrington, A. (2008). The cure within: A history of mind-body medicine. New York: Norton.

Rasmussen, N. (2008). On speed: The many lives of amphetamine. New York: NYU Press.

Tone, A. (2009). The age of anxiety: A history of America's turbulent affair with tranquilizers. New York: Basic Books.

9 798885 309745

Printed by Libri Plureos GmbH in Hamburg,
Germany